Hopelust

A Memoir

Gina Mast

www.Hopelust.com

Copyright © 2016 by Gina Mast

All rights reserved.

ISBN: 099822460X
ISBN-13: 9780998224602
Library of Congress Control Number: 2016917371
Hopelust, Wake Forest, NC

Dedication

For Luke, may your light continue to shine.
And for every heart that has been affected by *it* in any variety.

Contents

Author's Note · vii

Chapter 1	Journal Entry 2/21/14· 1
Chapter 2	It · 5
Chapter 3	Becoming the Lead Role in a Depressing Indie Flick · · · · · · · 9
Chapter 4	The Washer – Entering the Spin Cycle· · · · · · · · · · · · · · 15
Chapter 5	Putting "Color" Into Life ·24
Chapter 6	You Can Call Me Merle, Because I'm Feeling Haggard · · · · ·33
Chapter 7	Pinot Grigio is the New Coffee Creamer · · · · · · · · · · · · · 44
Chapter 8	Dreams· ·51
Chapter 9	The Dissolution of the Rescue Committee · · · · · · · · · · · ·55
Chapter 10	Clarity ·62
Chapter 11	Drip-Dry ·65
Chapter 12	So This is Trust?· ·85
Chapter 13	Where You Go, I'll Go ·91
Chapter 14	A Sense of Identity · 96
Chapter 15	Living a Life of Love· ·102
Chapter 16	Journal Entry 9/30/2016· ·109

Ending Note from the Author ·113

Author's Note

When writing this book, I copied actual entries from my journals. Each excerpt has a different formatting to distinguish it from the rest of the book. I left those entries mostly unrefined so that they are completely truthful and raw. I have changed the names of many people who were a part of my story in order to protect their anonymity. I also blurred out details in the images for this same reason.

Most people were baffled by the truth when they learned about my story because I hid *it*. I added images at the end of each chapter for several reasons: 1) to break down the stereotype of the typical person dealing with *it* and 2) to show how easily one can build a façade via social media. Things are rarely as they appear. So if other people's profiles make you feel like you're somehow missing the boat on life, I want you to know that this probably isn't the case. Everyone is fighting battles that don't make their profile. So if you're fighting a battle today, don't let this make you feel like you're alone in your fight.

Lastly, I hope that by pulling the curtain from in front of my heart and allowing others to peer inside, that those who need hope may find it. When I was in my darkest season, I'd have given anything for hope. Now that I found some, I want to pass it on.

Love, heart hugs, prayers and well wishes,

Gina

CHAPTER 1
Journal Entry 2/21/14

I've been there. I know the routine. Drinking to get drunk. Drinking to become numb. Drinking to ease the pain. You get home from work on a Friday afternoon. You bought a gallon of wine on your way home, hoping it'll be enough for the night. You look cleaned up from work. You hope the cashier isn't going to ask questions because you aren't throwing a party, you're medicating yourself for the night. You go to the young, naïve looking high school kid. He's not cynical enough to imagine one person finishing this jug by themselves. No, no, he's got grand plans. He believes that life gets easier after high school. High school is a battle, but it gets easier. Change your clothes. Draw the blinds, one by one. Because you don't want people who know you to see the lights on after dark. Because you will pass out on the couch later. You turn on the small lamps so that it'll be less noticeable from the outside, to anyone driving by. Maybe they'll think you forgot to turn them off. Surely they won't know that you are there. On the couch. Passed out.

You chug the first glass. Not a wine glass, but a 16 oz. water glass. You're in a hurry to get there. You're glad you didn't eat dinner because you'll get there quicker. You sit down to watch some TV. You start to get warm. It's working. You feel okay. Soon, you'll have another glass. You just somehow need more. You're okay, but you need a little more. You're gonna watch the awesome new movie on at 8 p.m. But it's not enough until you pass out. You black out. You close the world out. Why? It hurts. Everything hurts. Life hurts. Dreams seem impossible. Hope seems like an unquenchable thirst because you can never get enough of it.

You wake up. It's 7:30 p.m. You chug another full glass. You wake up. It's 11 p.m. Shit. You missed the fucking movie. You chug another glass or two. You wake up. It's 4 a.m. You chug another glass. You wake up. It's 7 a.m. You have a headache. You're shaky. You need one more glass to ease off. You have a small glass, which empties the bottle.

You beat yourself up. You're weak. You're pathetic. You're useless. You're nobody. You're a disgrace. You should be ashamed of yourself. How can you look at yourself? What if everyone knows? Do they know? Do they suspect it? Do they smell it on my breath? Am I eating enough garlic to cover it? This is getting expensive.

You need more. It's Saturday. How can you buy more at 7 a.m. without the cashier knowing? You try to clean. Or lay around. Or distract yourself until 10 or so because it's gotten so bad that you think normal people start buying it that early in the day. You get in the car, shaky from needing more. You drive to the different gas stations. You alternate. On Saturdays Exxon. On Sundays Kangaroo. On Sunday afternoons the one Rite Aid. On Sunday nights the other Rite Aid. On Tuesdays Target. On Wednesdays the small Harris Teeter. On Thursdays the big Harris Teeter. On Fridays Food Lion. On Friday nights the sketchy gas station a few miles further from home. You buy so many random groceries to mask the fact that you're there for wine. Just wine. Because it's early. You want them to think you're doing your grocery shopping for the week.

You come up for air and you buy more between pass-outs. You buy it in that stupid brown bag. You feel shame. You try to hide your shaky hands. They know. Everyone knows. They must see me walking to my car. They must see me hiding the trash. They must see my closet with bottles tucked here and there. They must see my dresser with more bottles. They must see me wrap the bottles inside boxes. Inside layers of grocery bags. Inside shoe boxes. Inside anything.

You wake up. It's Monday morning. Fuck. You're hung over. Your head hurts. You stand up. You're shaky. You struggle to get your balance. The weekend is glossed over. How can it be over? How can you stop shaking? You drink water. You chug some Red Bull. Some Diet Mountain Dew. You shower. You put your makeup on, hoping it'll help you look more put together. Your hand shakes while you apply it all, but it's more apparent when you apply your eyeliner. One foot in front of the other. "You have this. Get it the fuck together." You tell yourself.

On the drive to work, you're in a fog. You practice talking to yourself; you try to sound normal. Your voice still sounds a little like you're slurring. Or at least you think it does. Focus. Your brain feels foggy. Focus. I can't Focus. I can't Focus. I can't

You struggle through the day. You try to hide the shakes. But you know you can't. They see it. They all see it.

Gina Mast updated her profile picture.
January 21, 2014

That's me on the left. I have included screenshots from Facebook to highlight the sharp contrast between social media's portrayal of people and real life.

CHAPTER 2

It

I NEVER LIKED THE WORDS people used to label someone like me. They weren't pretty; they stung. And they made me more aware of the fact that I was acting like a worthless piece of shit. I didn't need anyone else to point this out; I already knew it. My conception of God knew how much I hated labels. When He showed up to ask me if I wanted healing, He referred to my condition without a label. He simply asked if I wanted Him to heal "it." So for the sake of not putting power on a label, I'm going to follow His lead and use *it* to refer to the ass beating alcohol gave me.

On a good day, the isolation I felt during my drinking career was unbearable. I lived in fear of being exposed. So much energy went into compartmentalizing my life to decrease the chances of people realizing the common theme: Gina had a drinking problem. I loved drinking; it was my favorite thing! I never really drank like others, though. I drank a lot and entered my Sleeping Beauty phase early on when I began to drink until I passed out.

My consumption of alcohol was like a car operating without brakes. Once I started drinking, I only gained speed, and I didn't stop until I crashed into a blackout or passed out. But this was okay because I was cute enough to get away with it. Alcohol made me cute. It turned me into a free spirit! I loved everyone. I was lighthearted and carefree. I was *just having fun*. I would stop being reckless when I was ready to settle down. I had the rest of my life to be responsible.

I don't know exactly when it happened but at some point, I stopped consuming alcohol and alcohol started consuming me. The thing that was once my escape somehow morphed into my own personal prison. I didn't realize that anything that I gave this much power to could eventually steal my power from me. My one-time crutch in social situations was now my legs that I needed simply to walk properly or function. I could not live without it. Trying not to drink was like trying to swim upstream; eventually, I surrendered and let the current wash me downstream. My downstream had a bottle trap that would hold me in it. And I would stay there, wallowing in defeat, until I got uncomfortable enough or saw a ray of hope. Then, I would try again.

Due to my disciplined nature, I was unable to comprehend and accept the fact that I wasn't able to control my drinking, which made stopping harder. I didn't realize that I would never gain the ability to do this. This is why the same hurdle tripped me every time I approached it. I like to think this was because I was determined and not because I was stupid. Over time, getting drunk lost its luster. The older I got, the more pathetic and sad it became. There was nothing cute about it anymore.

Alcohol stopped making me soft and sweet. Instead, it turned me into a malicious, erratic and unpredictable monster. I literally became another person. When I drank, it felt like I was crawling into the passenger seat of my own car and letting something else steer the wheel for me. My body was along for the ride, but my brain wasn't calling the shots, nor was it aware of what was going on most of the time. Every time I blacked out, some bad shit happened. It was always dark. Always.

The warm, almost euphoric, escape that lured me into drinking eventually stopped coming. When I was sober, I felt anxious, frustrated and distracted. I was always consumed with how to obtain some alcohol. When I finally had alcohol in my system, I felt like I could breathe again. Instead of being happy, I spent a lot of this time crying because I became depressed and alcohol contributed to even more depression.

When I was finally ready to stop, there was one small problem: I couldn't. Drinking was like one of those spiral water slides at amusement parks. One that went down further and further. There were no exits. And anytime I tried to climb back up to the top to get out the way I came in, I slipped and fell even further.

I didn't know anyone who had struggled with addiction. I knew that there was a monkey on my back, but I didn't know what I was looking at or what I was dealing with. I thought there was something in me that was broken. Everyone else was standing on the same ground as me; they were fine, yet I was drowning in quicksand. I didn't think anyone would understand. Because I didn't even understand.

More harmful than the uncomfortable circumstances *it* created, *it* wrecked my life by stealing my identity. Every fiber of my being thought *it* was my identity. *It* made me think I was powerless because powerlessness was what I saw when I looked in the mirror. I wore the shame that *it* created as though it were my skin, my freckles. *It* leached onto me like a giant tumor which contained a parasite that would suck the life out of me and devour every good thing in my life. My brokenness created this tumor, my frailty allowed it to sprout, and my weakness allowed it to thrive. Therefore, I was convinced that I deserved *it*.

What I didn't know then was that my experience with this horrific beast would one day be my most treasured blessing. I didn't know that the thing which devoured my old identity would lead me to discovering my true, powerful, unstoppable, unshakable identity. I didn't know the thing that shattered my world would become the foundation on which I would be rebuilt. I didn't know that this lie would be the one to expose every other lie I had believed about myself my entire life.

 ██████ ████ with ███████ ████ and **Gina Mast**.
February 16, 2013 · iOS

Valentine's soirée!
See Translation

Shortly after leaving this event, I blacked out. When I regained awareness, I was leaving a club at 2 a.m. I woke up the next morning with shredded nylons and bruises all over. I found out that I had thrown a full bottle of water at a guy I used to date because I was mad at him. Apparently, he saw how drunk I was and tried to get me to drink water so that I sober up. And instead of thanking him, I yelled at him and became aggressive. I also found out that I spent the night dancing and falling on the ground.

CHAPTER 3

Becoming the Lead Role in a Depressing Indie Flick

I THINK I LOOKED FAIRLY normal from the outside, or at least I put a lot of effort in appearing this way. I tried to stay active, and I made sure this was reflected in my social media accounts. I ran at least one half marathon a year. I frequented the gym. I was a young professional with full-time employment. I had obtained my bachelor's degree from Elon University by the age of twenty. I was disciplined. I worked hard. I had plenty of opportunities if I wanted them.

I grew up in a lower to middle-class family in northwestern Pennsylvania. I was the youngest of nine kids, born into an Amish family. My dad was a painter. He was the type that painted houses; not the creative, artsy kind. My mom worked harder than anyone I know; I'm grateful to have inherited a fraction of her work ethic. She was a cleaning lady but if you called her that, I hated you for it. She had a name. Sarah. And cleaning was just her job. You didn't dare call her a cleaning lady, even though that was what she did every day. This label was something that I fought but wore as my identity. I thought this made other people better than me.

When I was not in school, I had to go to work with my parents. So my evenings, weekends and summers consisted of cleaning and painting. There was nothing I hated more. I felt like a second-class citizen when I was scrubbing someone else's kitchen floor on my hands and knees or painting in stained work clothes. I never wanted people to find out what my parents' occupations were or that I helped them because I thought they would think I wasn't good enough. I didn't want people to think or know that we were poor. I measured my self-worth by my parents' income. At the time, I was a child. But I felt like the amount of money they earned indicated my level of worth.

My immediate family was tight-knit, to an extent. Our culture wasn't one that discussed feelings or showed our sentimental side. We all knew we loved each other, but we didn't say it out loud. When our hearts were hurting, we didn't really talk about it. So those feelings just kind of sat around and festered, unless they were cried out in secret. I didn't realize this was fertile soil for lies to sprout and thrive in. When things are kept a secret, nobody else can shed light on the truth. I avoided the sore spots in my heart because I didn't know how to work through them. Everyone was supportive, kind and loving.

My family left the Amish community when I was two. I attended a private Mennonite school until third grade when I transferred to a public school. Can we just stop for a minute and imagine a sheltered little ex-Amish kid who grew up without TV going to public school? I did not fit in. I was about as familiar with pop culture as I was fluent in Mandarin; I had zero exposure. My mom tried to help me blend in by buying me my first pair of jeans and other mainstream clothes, but my style was out of date. If you could call it a style.

This was the year I went to the movie theater for the first time. One of my brothers told me not to tell anyone at school that this was my first time or they would think I was a loser. This took me by surprise. So from here on, if I wasn't sure about something being socially acceptable, I wouldn't say it. I began tucking things into my increasingly expanding private closet.

I was a goofball around people who I knew well. But around strangers, I was a clam. Physically, I felt like something about me was just too big. I felt like I got in the way all the time. My head was a different size; I didn't fit into any room. I was skinny but I felt like one of those over-sized parade floats, gracelessly bopping into everything because I wasn't grounded. I knew that if anyone knew who I really was, they would know I didn't fit in so I did what any insecure person would do: I hid everything. This would become a pattern in my life. I thought that if I had grown up in a *normal* household, I would know how everything worked. So I rarely asked questions and I never asked for help. In our house, asking for help was a sign of weakness.

I was a people pleaser in order to gain acceptance. I never knew what I wanted myself; I had no life direction. I typically did what people told me to do. This made it easy to blame my lack of happiness on someone else and resent them for my life circumstances because it wasn't my damn fault; it was theirs.

I had a typical high school experience. At this point, I had become better at blending because I had been surrounded by *normal* people for a while. I had adapted to the lifestyle. I earned good grades, and I played soccer almost year round. I had plenty of girlfriends. We weren't the most popular kids, but we were cool enough. If our school had a cool-kid percentile, I might've fallen into the 75th, I think. But who really knows?

I did my best to maintain a goody-goody reputation. I was a combination of the new ideas I picked up from society and my parents' traditional values. I was scared to be anything other than a prude, sexually, and even my girlfriends eventually picked on me for it. When it came to substances, I didn't try anything stronger than weed. Those talks that they gave us in the school gymnasium actually worked on me. Well, the ones about hard drugs but I ignored the ones about pot and alcohol.

I experimented with cigarettes, weed, and booze. Cigarettes weren't appealing, and weed made me paranoid, but alcohol worked just perfectly. I belonged in the secret rebellious cool kid club. I smoked pot for the first time at thirteen and I smoked it a handful of times in high school. Not many people outside of my close group of friends knew this; I did not want to be classified as a pothead.

I drank when I could, which was about once or twice a month. I wasn't afraid of people knowing I drank because it wouldn't earn a bad reputation. If anything, it gave me cool-kid points. The first few times, I didn't drink much because I was scared of getting sick. I thought that was the worst thing that happened when people drank. Drinking gave me something that I hadn't possessed before: courage. It made me bold. It made me funnier and better all around.

My involvement in sports delayed *it* from hitting me sooner. I only drank when I was with other people; never alone. There was maybe one time that I tried to mix vodka in my Jell-O back when we still used ICQ (like AOL Instant Messenger but older) and I wanted to chat with people. I didn't actually feel any effects at this time. Plus, my parents were playing Scrabble in the next room. So I didn't feel sad-alone. I felt rebellious and sneaky. I drank on the occasional weekend and when I went to my first few college parties.

During my senior year, I blacked out for the first time at my best friend's New Year's party. I didn't do this intentionally. In fact, I hadn't even known it was possible. I thought people just made up blackouts cause they were buzzing, did something dumb, and didn't want to be held accountable for their actions. I thought people always knew what they were doing. Anyways, I had to work earlier that night, so I slammed liquor to catch up with everyone else. But then I passed everyone after I finished dancing on the living room furniture. And passed out hugging the toilet.

Due in part to my upbringing and in part to my resources, college was on me. If I chose to attend, I would have to pick up the tab. So even though I graduated from college early, I had raked in a substantial amount of student loan debt. Since my family wasn't convinced that higher education was worth the money, I had to prove otherwise. Even though I was at a job that I hated, I had too much pride to admit this out loud. Instead of openly discussing how I felt when I graduated, I sucked it up and hid it in the secret closet where I hid the lump sum of the student loan debt I had incurred. I assumed I was the only college grad experiencing this confusion and disappointment of entering the real world. I didn't want to be the only person who didn't have my shit together, so I kept it quiet.

I was unprepared for life, largely due to unrealistic expectations. I thought I'll be happy when a) I finish high school, b) I finish college, c) I start working, etc. Happiness was always a destination in the future. But here, there was no future. This was it. And I was not happy.

My job wasn't satisfying. I had a large amount of responsibility in a high-stress environment. Since I always sought fulfillment externally, I thought the problem was my job. I wanted to find something more fun but I was scared to move because of my monthly student loan bills. I couldn't afford to hop around between jobs and risk missing a paycheck.

I wasn't sure if it was the stress that I was keeping to myself or my screwed up insides that made me feel discontent in my long-term relationship with my college sweetheart. I felt restless and frustrated, but I was scared to walk away from the main thing that gave me a sense of stability; Matt made me feel less alone. Life was a river and I was grasping for things to cling to in order to stay afloat.

I had the lead role in one of those depressing indie flicks. Driving into Louisburg, the town where my office was, made my stomach sink. Mostly because it felt like my hometown, good old Meadville. I was in that same uncomfortable place that I'd spent all of my life wanting to leave, just in a different state. I wasn't satisfied with life but I didn't know what to do. I didn't know how to change things. Life had played a big cruel joke on me. I started withering up inside.

To deal with the stress and disappointment of entering the real world, I started drinking evenings so that I could relax and sleep. Drinking fixed everything. All of the feelings and concerns I had about missing the boat were washed away by alcohol. I had discovered a bandage and a shortcut to get rid of anxiety!

It turns out, this salve was a great way to cope with pain; a breakup in 2010 and again in 2011 fueled my drinking. Alcohol made me feel depressed after a bender weekend. To get rid of that depression, I drank more. I became increasingly depressed and as a result, I began to isolate myself. Loneliness made me want to drink more because I didn't like feeling alone. If I was sad, I drank. If I was angry, I drank. If I was stressed, I drank. If I was happy, I drank. If I had no reason, I drank.

Sarah and Amir

This is what a lot of my evenings looked like after college. I had lots of people around me and plenty of family to keep me company.

CHAPTER 4

The Washer – Entering the Spin Cycle

AT FIRST, I ONLY DRANK evenings. There was nothing wrong with a few glasses of wine with dinner; it made me feel glamorous, sophisticated, and mature. I never enjoyed the taste of wine, but I enjoyed the feeling it brought me. I inherited the tendency to chug things from my dad. Especially when it came to nutritional supplements and smoothies, I would gulp it down to get it over with. Naturally, because I didn't have an appreciation for the taste of wine, I had to remind myself to sip it, thinking I might eventually learn to enjoy it. I didn't. I always wanted to straight guzzle it to get the result faster. But I could play along over dinner and try to pace with whoever else was there so that I could appear as though I was enjoying it.

When the relationship with my college sweetheart found its demise in early 2010, I used wine to help cope with my broken heart. I knew that I was using it as a tool but I didn't see anything wrong with this. My main thought was: how can I get through tonight? And the answer was always wine.

This breakup was particularly challenging to work through because Matt was my rock. Since I had transferred into Elon and met him at the very beginning, he was my college experience. In large, he was my identity. He was Mr. Outgoing and I was his Ms. Quiet, but I was okay with this. I liked being able to rely on him to carry conversations and break me out of my shell. I invested most of my time at school into him, so I didn't build many other lasting relationships. I had buddies, but I didn't get as close to the girls as I might have had he not been in the picture.

I never felt like I fit in or belonged at Elon. Ironic, the overused line on campus was Elon: Where you bELONg! Coming from a small farm in Northwestern PA, I was completely unprepared for the Elon experience. I drove onto campus in my 1997 Camry and parked in lots where it seemed like every other car was a BMW, Mercedes or Lexus. I was one of the few students who didn't come from a privileged home. I was there on my own tab and on student loans, so I felt like I didn't deserve to be there. I didn't have clothes to dress the part. I tried. I bought J. Crew and Banana Republic pieces at the outlets but I wasn't fooling anyone.

I didn't want to accept the fact that I wasn't like everyone else. I didn't want to live my role authentically and embrace my roots. I didn't want to accept my differences. I piled who I was into the closet and tried to set up a bookcase in front of the door. I filled the shelves with things I deemed presentable and pretty. I didn't complain about living on Hot Pockets and Diet Coke because I didn't want anyone to know that I couldn't afford to pay extra for a meal plan. At this point, my parents were successful and back on their feet. However, they didn't think it fair to help out with more than occasional gas and grocery money since they didn't put my older siblings through school. They did pay for my car insurance and my cell phone, which helped.

The good thing about me graduating at the age of twenty was that I couldn't buy alcohol by myself. This was my saving grace. That, and the fact that I was busy with school work. I didn't drink often because I didn't have time. Drinking didn't have its claws under my skin yet. When I drank, I usually experienced blackouts or brownouts. But I wasn't drinking to the point of passing out. College gave me a free pass to binge drink. My drinking patterns flew under the radar. Alcohol was a buffer to ease social anxiety. And it worked every time; it made me enough. I didn't have huge consequences other than those awful hangovers.

After college graduation, I lived in Raleigh and Matt lived an hour away in Greensboro. A few months after starting his job, his company let him go to NYC for a rotation. He had wanted to live there but I think he was scared to make the move alone. He tried to convince me to move there so he could stay permanently. I might have if it weren't for the weight I carried from my student loans and from my family's disapproval of the idea.

I was in denial that he was behaving strangely. He was able to fly me up for free every two weeks, but he didn't. He transferred our communication over to his second phone. I had a dream that he was being disloyal but I discarded it as fear. I ignored him changing his grooming habits. One night after we said goodnight, I called him back even though he had gone to bed because I couldn't sleep. I heard a girl's voice in the background. He then told me he had gone out for drinks with Ashley, a fellow Elon grad. Why was he hiding a friend? I didn't know. I pushed past these things because I didn't want to believe that he didn't love me anymore. Then he started sending me job postings in random places like Oklahoma. I finally started seeing the picture: he was afraid to break up with me. If realizing this would've been a race, I'd have come in last place. Sometimes I wonder how I earned my Bachelor's in three years. But love will do that to you. Upon facing the truth, I broke things off and set him free.

I didn't want to let go of the security that this relationship provided even though I sometimes had a flutter in my stomach when I passed a stranger who wasn't him. I had lost my virginity to him. He was my best friend. He knew where I came from and he accepted me for me. He knew the real Gina. I let him further into my closet than anyone before him. Realizing that he saw what was inside and wasn't interested in staying was a hard pill to swallow. I couldn't fault him for this. We were both young.

I thought that I was no longer desirable because I had chosen him over keeping my purity ring the summer before my senior year. I had been coached from an early age that guys don't like easy girls. I thought that he was "the one" simply because I wanted him to be the one. I wanted to settle down young and live a calm life. He was just a good friend but at the time, I couldn't distinguish between being in love and loving someone. I continued to wear the ring that I had received for my 16th birthday because I thought it wasn't cheating if I would marry him. I thought I waited until I met the man I would marry. But when we broke up, I came clean. And I bought a replacement ring that I wore on that finger as a symbol of my strength and independence.

Only, I wasn't independent. I didn't want to be single. I didn't want to be like the girls in romantic comedies. I didn't want to date around. I wanted nothing to do with any of it. I wanted security. I wanted to be married yesterday. But life had other plans, as it often does.

I tried to make the most of this time and I sought out fun. This was the first time I was finally old enough to party legally. So this meant I could actually go out and drink at bars without sneaking booze in the bathroom. I didn't go out often but when I did, I went big. I might black out but I stayed out of trouble. I never drove drunk, I cabbed home or got rides from nice people. I used to take a picture of the license plate and text it to my brother in California so that he would know who to look for if something happened to me.

I ran off the hangovers the next morning though because I wasn't living alone. I had to try to hide the mess I'd made the night before and my resilient 21-year-old body cooperated. I started waking up around 2 a.m. on nights when I finished an entire bottle of wine. Pounding heart, pounding headache and wide awake. I made my first proclamations not to drink during this time. Of course, I had guidelines for the drinking because I was far from being willing to give it up altogether.

I had no idea who I was. I dabbled with painting, but I was afraid to venture out anywhere. I finally found the courage to join a gym (I told you I had anxiety). I hung out mostly with my family. I had three sisters in the area and they were all married with kids so I never felt like I fit in; I felt like the third wheel. I tried to help out by decorating for birthday parties and spoiling my nieces and nephews, but I really wanted a family of my own. I wanted someone who would take me under their wing and help me come out of my shell. I wanted someone to pave the way for me. I waited in my tower for a year. I thought that Prince Charming was going to show up and find me. I know this was naïve but I wanted God to spare me the process of sorting through the assholes.

Since I had been introduced to the idea of God as a child, I only talked to Him when I wanted something. I thought He created the world and only sometimes stepped in to help out. The only "interactions" I had with Him were when He gave me accurate dreams about things. But I hadn't had any major prayers answered. He was my last resort. I would do everything I knew to do, then when I was in a jam, I would yell out to the big guy upstairs to come bail me out. When things didn't go my way, I doubted Him. My beliefs went around like a merry-go-round. When things were good, I believed in God. When things were bad, I doubted His power or His intentions.

Anyways, I didn't want to date because I knew that would require vulnerability and I knew I could potentially, and would likely, have my heart broken again. I started running every day, exercising, and getting myself ready for Prince Charming.

About the same time as the college sweetheart's breakup, my friend's brother moved in from California. He was tall, dark and handsome. He perfectly fit the bill. If I could have dreamt up a soul mate, he would've been it. He was laid back, he was outgoing, and he was kind. He was my perfect counterpart.

It took him almost a year to muster up the courage to ask me out. While I was waiting, I had multiple dreams about him. When we were dating, the accuracy of the dreams was confirmed. I had known he had never truly loved someone prior to me. I took the accurate dreams as a sign from God that he was my soul mate. Why else would God reveal these things to me? I let go of the reservations that I had; I was no longer petrified. The dreams gave me the courage to open up to him and let him inside my closet. I felt safe with him; he was gentle. I loved everything about him, down to his hands. He had those rugged manly-man hands.

Our relationship progressed quickly. I started staying at his house within months. Of course, since I was a people pleaser, I hid this from my traditional/conservative parents and as much of my family as I could. I was avoiding judgment and criticism, and I knew my parents wouldn't approve. I thought we were going to get married, so I felt comfortable with the idea. We were grownups, and we knew what we wanted.

I loved living there. He was wonderful and perfect. I had someone to cook for, or at least I tried. I was awful in the kitchen. If I had chosen healthier ingredients, I would have been a viable competitor for Nutrisystem; my meals made portion control a cinch. I loved having wine when I made dinner.

> I discovered that there are only four things a beginner cook needs: 1) hot sauce 2) A1 sauce 3) cheese or 4) wine. If none of the first three things can fix it, the fourth one will. Consumed separately, of course.

I drank every night but he did too. He drank normally. I drank a lot but most of the time it went unnoticed. There were several occasions when I blacked out after margarita night at the local Mexican restaurant. Then once at a wedding, he told me on the way home that he didn't like when I drank that much around him. I think I embarrassed him at the wedding and I felt embarrassed of myself because I didn't remember anything. I hoped he would forget about it ASAP. I just wanted to sweep it under the rug.

He once told me that he mentioned my drinking to his dad. I guess I was mean during a blackout, but he said it was okay since I apologized. The key here is that it should've been a red flag that he thought the drinking was problematic, given that his father would go on to die from alcoholism and it had plagued him for years, but I didn't take notice. Instead, I tried to just not blackout. When I say I tried to not blackout, I tried to drink normally. Since I lacked the ability to drink normally, there wasn't a change. When we went anywhere, I would drink and he would drive. But I thought it was his job to drive because he was the man and he was supposed to take care of me. I didn't consider that I was always the one drinking more.

During late fall of 2011, the walls of our castle came tumbling down. There was a misunderstanding between my brothers-in-law and him involving work and he became offended. The pain and bitterness this caused made it hard for me to spend time with my family. If I went to family functions, I felt guilty for leaving him behind. If I didn't attend family functions, I felt guilty for ditching them. It was apparent that he wanted me to choose him or them, and I chose them.

I was completely devastated, even though it was my choice. When I had the dreams which were confirmed, I thought that was God indicating that this was the man I would spend my life with. So when shit hit the fan, I got really mad at God. I blamed Him for setting me up for heartbreak. I thought He had abandoned me. I kept asking Him to fix the relationship and He didn't. I clung to the hope that He would restore and repair this relationship because I was certain that he was "the one" for me. But He didn't.

Despite my pleading and the nights I lay awake crying, I was alone again. My heart ached. Disappointment and rage filled me simultaneously. I started drinking larger quantities due to my increased tolerance. I was drinking about three-fourths of a bottle of wine a night. I wasn't trying to drink; I was trying to be okay with life. I was trying to cope with my heart hurting. I felt like I had lost my home. He loved me, he doted on me and treated me like a princess; it was a fairytale. Why was it ruined?

We tried to reconcile several times, but we never gained any ground. I knew that if Bayn was the right guy for me, God would work it out. But I thought that he was for me and I didn't understand why God wasn't working it out. Must be God didn't give a shit about me. Here I am again, as a last resort asking Him to bail me out and He isn't showing up to help me. But He has to show up! He's the one that gave me the dreams. Am I somehow unworthy of being helped? Am I undeserving of Him cleaning up my mess again? Is it because I sinned? Did I goof up by engaging in pre-marital hanky panky? I thought we were going to get married so I didn't see the harm in this. Did I disqualify myself from being blessed? Does He even hear me? I'm screaming at the top of my lungs. No, God. You hear me. You will fix this. You've got to fix this!

I kept thinking God would turn the ship around. But He wasn't.

11/4/11 The last two months have been hell. I used to think people who are strong are lucky because I've always considered myself to be weak. Strength isn't fuck. Strength is forged through sleepless nights, heartbreaks and surviving gut-wrenching moments that leave you unable to breathe (not in the good way).

It's forged in situations where you lose everything but your hope (you've lost your mind, your feet tremble, your hands shake, your eyes can't see through the saline waterfalls projecting from them). Your friends fall away like snow melting in the spring. You feel like Jim Carey in Bruce Almighty (calling God a mean kid with a big magnifying glass, cursing him out because you're the runt) and life just looks like my sister Josi would say "shit hath hitteth the fan."

Strength comes from those who face hardships; who choose to overcome, who throw in the victim towel and get back up. Maybe with a small limp, they keep trudging. They say life has seasons. I've been through winters before but this feels like fucking hurricane season.

I wanted a fresh start. I had outgrown my prior home; I returned to it a new person and that person could no longer be contained within those walls. In December of 2011, I moved to Cameron Village, a neighborhood within walking distance of downtown Raleigh. I was living unsupervised for the first time since college.

I was crying myself to sleep most nights. Of course I tried not to let anyone know. I could still act like a goofball; alcohol helped me mask my feelings. I felt panicked, forsaken by God, and abandoned.

CHAPTER 5

Putting "Color" Into Life

1/27/2012 The bad thing about a night out drinking: there is nothing you can do about buyer's remorse. Unfortunately, there are no return policies, credits or exchanges.

Trust me, I tried it. I discovered a fraudulent charge on my credit card on a Monday. My wrath was quickly transformed into embarrassment when I learned that the charge I was disputing was, in fact, a street hot dog vendor.

By February of 2012, the newness and distraction of the move had worn off and I found myself lonely and missing my old routine. The small apartment I lived in felt too big. It felt empty, even though I had a roommate. My room felt empty, even though I was inside of it with lots of things. At night, when I could no longer distract myself from the giant pit in my stomach, I drank some wine.

Earlier on in life, I had sensed this void but I usually found distractions. I had deadlines to work on, especially in school. I would look for my situation to change and I could tough out anything short-term. But this void was big. It was the size of the world and it wasn't going anywhere. It filled my chest with fire. My roommate often emptied the candy dishes at night and I often emptied the wine bottle(s). I thought we were doing the same thing, just responding differently. Wine was like a warm, cozy blanket that soothed me.

Who was I? Independent from a boyfriend or anything else, who was Gina? I could be anyone now that I had a fresh start but I didn't know who

I wanted to become. I was so lost that I couldn't even choose what groceries to buy. Part of me wanted to venture out but most of me wanted to go home again to Bayn.

Only home wasn't there anymore. I knew there was no future at that home. And I knew I wasn't supposed to go back. But I felt like a kid living in an apartment complex. I missed living in a house. I missed weekend projects and painting and remodeling. I missed knowing who I was hanging out with every night and having someone to cook dinner for. More than anything, I missed the feeling of knowing who I would spend my future with. I felt sad and lonely so I drank. If my circumstances would change, then I'd become happy. And when I became happy, I'd stop drinking. But my circumstances weren't changing.

I registered for my first half-marathon, and I was running every day. I also started putting myself out there to meet people. I worked to reconnect with college friends and with others who had dropped by the wayside during my consuming relationships. I wanted to establish female friendships because I knew that was the one thing that I needed to do differently this time around. I knew that men would come and go and that I should focus on making some good girlfriends.

Shortly after moving, I ran into a neighbor and had one of those "this is who I'm going to marry" thoughts. I'm not sure exactly what it was about him, but I realized that there was someone who could make me feel more excited than I had felt about Bayn. I wanted a man like this to sweep me off my feet. I hated waiting for one. I knew I should focus on building female relationships. However, I wanted the security blanket that a relationship provided.

An acquaintance of my sister ran into me one day by chance. She knew a lot about me, despite not knowing me. She seemed to think I heard from God all the time. She said that I was kind, funny, and peaceful. This almost pissed me off. What a joke. I was the furthest thing from peaceful. According to her, people spoke me into becoming a worrier but I wasn't actually a worrier. She went on to say that I had recently met a man who was interested in me. She laughed and said I wouldn't figure out how, but when I least expected it, he would approach me. God was supposedly going to use the situation with this guy to show me that He had me all along.

How did she know that I doubted whether or not God had me? I felt excited but confused. I did not feel peaceful. I constantly felt anxious, stressed, and uptight. I wanted to hope what she said was true, the same way you might hope that a favorable psychic forecast is true, but I was scared to be disappointed. I asked God how I could know if her information was credible. I tried to use the peace litmus test: keep it if it brings me peace and discard it if it doesn't, but I struggled to distinguish between hope and peace. I thought it brought me peace. But maybe I just wanted hope.

It was around this time that I was introduced to the magical cure for a hangover. The trick was to have one drink of whatever I had consumed the night before. I drank wine, so if I had a glass of wine, my hangover either went away entirely or it was dulled. I would have one innocent serving of alcohol to get rid of the hangover. Then I would have one more. And one more. And one more. When I started drinking, I rarely stopped until I passed out or ran out of booze. So this was also when I started day drinking on weekends.

My roommate left for a few months, so I had the apartment to myself. I hid most of my alcohol consumption from her because she didn't drink. Of course, if you compared how much I was drinking with someone who didn't drink, it seemed like a lot. But that was because she didn't drink. A normal person would've drank more like me, she was the exception. Since I didn't have to hide it as much, I would just start drinking and pass out whenever I pleased. Wake up, get more booze, and do it again. I was able to show up if I needed to be somewhere. I was still able to stop drinking a few drinks in. I just hated to, so unless I had a good reason, I didn't. At this point, it was more of a strong urge than a necessity.

When I had to choose between drinking and doing other stuff, drinking almost always won for the simple fact that it was easier and it provided a sense of comfort. If I could drink and do an activity, I was good. If there was no alcohol, I probably wasn't interested. Drinking put color into my life. Sobriety was drab and gray and boring. I wanted a life of color! I wanted excitement. And I also wanted peace. Booze brought me those things. It also muffled out those awful scrambling worries of "It's a Friday! Every person in the universe is having fun. You need to find something fun to do right now or you're going to miss out on everything."

Starting somewhere new is hard. Talking to strangers when you have anxiety is almost as painful as sticking your hand over a fire. It's just constant discomfort. I would've done anything to make this easier. Alcohol made this easier; it was my go-to.

I was born a controller; I always tried to maintain control of situations. Alcohol was something that I used to cope with the uncontrollable factors in life. It helped me control the stress that arose from life. It turned me into a peaceful hippie. It masked out the anxiety I felt and it made me happy. Alcohol was my escape; it was the solution to every problem I had.

I knew that if I was hiding it, it wasn't normal. But I thought I belonged to this secret solution club. And I felt bad for anyone else who hadn't discovered my club. Because it was wonderful. It was so easy!

I had headaches every single day and would often imagine what would happen if I just ran my car off the road on my drive to work. It was torture to sit in an office all day when my head was killing me. Otherwise, my body was resilient. My stomach aches weren't awful. I could gulp down some Gatorade, eat Subway and pop a few Excedrin with some extra Red Bull and I was good to go. I had no problems hiding this. I just put on a brave face and toughed it out.

Being tired was my normal. I was staying up late at night drinking. I loved wasting time on social media. Thank God they created the activity log feature. I used it for damage control every morning so that I could clean up after myself without leaving tracks. I also went out on weeknights.

2/24/12 Got kicked out of the Hibernian. A duet was singing. I took over when one of them left for a cigarette break. I danced and sang. A girl [in the audience] made a snide remark. So I flipped her off with both hands. I wouldn't have known this but a guy I met that night texted to ask me on a date. I said yes. But only cause I needed to know what happened that night. I "came to" outside when I was crying. I knew I wasn't allowed back in but nobody told me why. I was embarrassed so I went home.

Not only was I poisoning my body, I was also losing sleep. I tried not to have the morning drink during the week so I would run instead. I started skipping morning runs as my drinking progressed. But I did get evening runs in so I was maintaining my façade.

I honestly wasn't very concerned with long-term health problems at this point. Yes, I was drinking every day and most nights I had an entire bottle of wine, but I thought my body was made to handle it. I was concerned about my weight, though, so I started lifting weights and exercising more to compensate for the empty calories. I also started trying to eat healthier because it was all hanging onto my stomach. It wasn't noticeable enough to set off any red flags.

I tried limiting my drinking to weekends but I rarely made it the entire week. Maybe I had a bad day. Or maybe it was already Thursday and that was basically the weekend. And Wednesday was almost Thursday. And Mondays were a free pass because I had to ease off of benders and I had to cope with the stress from blackouts that happened. It never lasted. Maybe a day or a week. But I always fell off.

7/4/12 Father, fix the drinking issue please.

I was aware that I had lost some discipline with drinking. I had no idea that I was just going to keep losing control progressively. I had done research on alcohol abuse and I thought that the researchers had sticks up their asses and that they were boring. I didn't think their statements applied to me; I liked to live outside their boring guidelines. Since I was mostly disciplined, I hated the fact that I wasn't able to be disciplined with drinking.

My cute neighbor, the hottie, moved out of my building in September and was gone. I was confused. Every time that I thought he was out of the picture, I would have another dream about him. It is strange how much I felt like I knew him from having conversations with him in dreams. Even though I didn't understand it, I thought the dreams were accurate. So I waited. I dated other people all year long, but I always broke things off because I wanted to be available when he came back for me, like the lady said he would.

I had a bunch of dreams about him that laid out a story line. In the one, he had come to my parent's house back home. But then I had to go upstairs because a monkey had jumped on my back and was fighting me. It took me a while to wrestle off the monkey. When I finally wrestled it off, it was dark outside and he had been long gone. I was walking into the living room to close the blinds when I saw him come up the driveway. He had been at the home improvement store and he had brought two light fixtures and a small sink for my family's house. He also brought some shoes. The thought occurred to me that maybe the monkey was my blackouts, but I didn't know. In the dream, I asked my sister, "How could he know what we needed in our house if he's never seen the inside of it?" And she replied with, "Did it ever occur to you that he has visions too?" I was private regarding my beliefs about God so never in my wildest dreams would I have thought I would find another person who experienced my same dreams or interactions with God. If this was the case, if he did hear from God, then God would bring him back. God would keep him for me.

I was someone who cared about what other people thought more than almost anything. I found out about some things I did during blackouts that made me cringe for years. Flashbacks were horrific to relive. Most of the worst things I did were told to me after blackouts. Sometimes I'm not sure if it was worse to wonder what I had done or find out that I had made a complete and utter fool of myself. I am familiar with the warm flush that floods the face and cheeks. I spent so many days walking around with my head down because I was horrified that someone would recognize me from a blackout. I was told that I became belligerent and mean. I said things I would never say to people. Then when I "came to," feeling depressed and overflowing with self-hate, the very people who I needed the most had been filleted open by me the night before.

People think that alcohol is always a truth serum. Sometimes it made me more honest, but other times, I said things that I didn't agree with. I would reflect on these things when I was by myself, and get really honest with myself.

In my heart of hearts, I did not feel this way. Why would I say these things during a blackout? I don't know.

> 6/20/13 I had two dreams last night. In the one, I was held hostage: I was on a sidewalk and was gunned down with a group of people. Cops came and the bad guy tried to run; we all did. Somehow the cops thought it was a protest and had orders to arrest us. I saw a cop and cried for help. He said he wasn't allowed to and advised me to run and hide. Ran past two cops and the third got me and tackled me. I was arrested. Later it was cleared up. [This is exactly what blackouts felt like; being held hostage by alcohol when you didn't know you were involved in the crime.]

I hated hiding. I was always hiding. I wore a black Under Armor hat to the gym. I told myself it would prevent people from potentially recognizing me. But I just wanted to fucking hide. I was terrified to learn of things I had done (like the time I blacked out at Legends, the LGBT bar. Danced on the stage and poles all night and woke up to bruises EVERYWHERE). I didn't want to know who saw me asleep on the chair outside of Coglin's before my friends scooped me up to get me home. Or who saw my best friend's boyfriend load me into his car in a headlock because I was belligerently yelling at him for no apparent reason. I didn't want to know because I couldn't face the shame. So I drank to ease off that anxiety. But when I had to show up somewhere without the booze, like at the gym, I felt like humble pie. My ego was on the ground covered in scrapes and bruises, dragging around somewhere behind me. When I royally screwed up and I knew people looked down on me, it taught me mercy.

When I had to walk around after finding out I had done something foolish, I learned humility. I know how hard it is to show up when everyone saw me crying the night before, talking about how I was a loser. Or knowing that I peed myself while I was passed out somewhere. It made me uptight but it also made me soft. I was the mess. I was the chaos that I so harshly judged in my younger days. I started to understand that even though I was doing my very best to be a responsible person, my best effort wasn't enough.

New Year's Resolution 2013: No alcohol

When people were warm in spite of these things, and kind enough to act like it didn't happen, I learned grace. This melted my icy heart. These instances would wash warm love into my frigid body. This was nourishment to my hungry soul. I just wanted love. This is exactly how Jesus was when He showed up in my life. He didn't care what I had done; there was never any shame. I think that I was so busy yelling self-hate things to myself that it made it hard for me to hear Him sometimes. But He was there all along, trying to show me He loved me.

Gina Mast in ♦ Playa del Carmen, Mexico.
October 28, 2012 · ⊙ · 👥

"Wishing I was knee deep in the water somewhere
Got the blue sky breeze and it don't seem fair
Only worry in the world is the tide gonna reach my chair
Sunrise there's a fire in the sky
Never been so happy... See More

  Ironic that the lyrics I chose for the caption include "Never been so happy..." because I was far from happy. I went on this trip with a girl I tolerated simply because I wanted the opportunity to travel. Her dad was a drinker so she let me know that she picked up on other people who had drinking issues. This meant I couldn't even get drunk while I was there.

CHAPTER 6

You Can Call Me Merle, Because I'm Feeling Haggard

I THINK IT WAS SOMEWHERE in 2013 when the shaking began. Initially, it was just after bender weekends. When I say bender weekend, I mean a few consecutive days of heavy alcohol consumption. Kind of like the opening journal entry. Eventually, the hangovers disappeared some and the shakes emerged in their place. I couldn't hide the shakes. At first, I would try to hide the shakes under a layer of coffee along with the line "Man, I had too much coffee! I'm so jittery!" This was during the time when the company that owned my apartment building decided it'd be a good idea to put a sports bar on the first floor. This is a dream come true for someone having issues with *it*. When I was already drunk but not drunk enough to pass out, I could walk downstairs then find my way home in blackouts. I rarely recalled putting myself to bed.

6/17/13 I never journaled about Frederick. Odd. We were friends. One morning (Saturday of Saint Patty's day parade), I woke up and he was [using my unconscious/asleep body in a way it shouldn't have been used. As I lay there, helpless and unaware, he accessed my body and trespassed into my temple.] I was disoriented. Confused. I didn't know how I got there. It was 6:22 a.m. I cried. I yelled at him. I told him there is nothing he can do to comfort me. I took the back stairwell for days. Weeks. I confronted him in person. I cried. I hate *him. I got tested for everything but I still want to gut him. I've realized I didn't remember being happy in a long time. I want to feel peaceful and secure.*

I remember going to his apartment to watch his Game of Thrones DVD the night before. I remember sitting in the living room. I remember something about 17 or 27 year old scotch. I remember chugging some because that's what I did with alcohol. I probably had wine before we hung out. In fact, I'm certain I did. That's why I liked hanging out there; I didn't have to drive anywhere. I think I remember making out in the living room.

Due to the passage of time, I think I'd have had to be passed out. But I don't know. I didn't know how I got into his bed. I didn't know where my clothes were. I went home, I drank some wine. I drove to one Rite Aid to buy a Plan B and then I drove to Harris Teeter to get a few bottles of wine. Then I got in the shower; I'm not sure if I cried. I was confused. I called my ex who was still living in NYC. I wanted to talk to someone familiar and there wasn't anyone else I could call that early on a Saturday. I needed some comfort. I didn't tell him what was wrong. I just talked to him.

After that, I had recurring nightmares about the scene repeating itself. There were slight variations but it was the same confused and helpless feeling of being exposed and betrayed. I couldn't be around him. I was parking in a different parking lot and climbing five flights of stairs so that I could avoid running into him in the elevator.

After confronting him in person and getting some of my rage out, he said that I was brave to talk to him and that he didn't know I had blacked out. I don't know if I was unconscious or not when he started penetrating my body and I'll never know. He sounded like he felt bad but I don't know whether or not it was sincere. I just wanted him to go away. He was supposed to move out of state, so I counted down the days to the end of his lease.

I have tried to forgive him. It's been a process. Sometimes I think I will be okay and I see the human in him. Sometimes I think he has a heart, like anyone else, and I think that he could never have done something that malicious intentionally. Other times my stomach reels and I wish I could see him standing on the road and just plow my car through his body. Because my fists couldn't hit him hard enough. I wonder if I could've passed for semi-normal to him. I always thought my drunkenness was more apparent to others. Is it possible that it wasn't that apparent to him? Is it possible that even though I was unconscious, that I was actually moving in my sleep? I don't know.

I was lonely. I was there because I didn't want to be alone and I thought it was safe. I wanted to curl up on someone's couch. I wanted to have a human near. I was sad and depressed. I just didn't want to feel alone. I didn't have intentions of that happening. I just wanted some company. I knew what I wanted, and I knew what I didn't want. What could I do about something that had already been done? I didn't have a leg to stand on and I sure as hell didn't want someone to expose my drinking. *It* was wrecking my life.

Prior to getting the blood test results back, I cried and cried. I tried to apologize to younger Gina for not protecting her. I endangered her. I deserved hell but she didn't. She was sweet and innocent. I was a binge drinker who was haggard and forlorn and ugly and pathetic. But she was none of those things. She didn't deserve this. She didn't deserve to feel like she wasn't safe. She didn't deserve to feel dirty like that. She didn't want that to happen. Drunk Gina put her in harm's way. And Drunk Gina was mad at herself for it.

It was during times like these where I felt as though I couldn't talk to anyone because they wouldn't understand, that I would talk to Jesus. Just Him. And I would ask Him to preserve me and protect me. Knowing I didn't deserve help, I asked anyway. And it was during these times where He let me know that He heard me, He loved me, and I mattered to Him. I used to think that I had to ask someone more righteous than me to pray for stuff. Cause I thought God wouldn't hear my prayers because I wasn't worthy enough. But this taught me that I was worthy and that even if it was just my little voice pleading, He came through. Slowly, I was coming to understand His love.

I could've talked to Frederick, but he wouldn't have offered any comfort. The one person I could vent to was the person who had hurt me. I grilled him about his health and he didn't have a history of getting checked. From his interactions with me, I doubt he was a cautious individual. This situation scared me. I didn't want to be around anyone anymore because I felt like nobody could be trusted. He hadn't used protection. I wasn't on birth control.

I was crawling out of my skin. I had to wait the recommended three-month minimum to run the blood tests to check for STIs, including HIV. I was petrified. I felt a fear that nothing could numb. I had gone to a yoga class at the gym because I was trying to find a sense of peace. I was laying in Savasana at the end of class the first time I saw Jesus. In a vision, I was under a tree in a meadow, next to a wilderness. I was sitting and Jesus was sitting beside me. He was love. I felt pure and safe and loved. I felt soft. Due to the presence of third person in the vision, I had a peaceful knowing that my test results would come back negative. I began to weep. I had been hardening myself to appear okay after the incident and upon feeling Jesus' love, my hard exterior melted. He saw me; He saw everything that had happened, yet He didn't look at those things. He looked at my heart. He saw my sweet intentions. He saw young Gina inside Drunk Gina. He was beckoning her to come out. I was overwhelmed. I got up and walked out of the yoga room, tears streaming down my face. Then I stopped at the store, got wine, went home and drank.

> 6/25/13 Lately I've been feeling like my options are more and more narrow. Idk if I'd hurt the family less by getting rid of myself or by continuing my lifestyle.
>
> I want to change. I want to be happy and peaceful. I feel like trash. I feel more isolated than ever. I feel so, so alone. Please fix me. Rebuild me. Mold me. It's been so long. I don't want to live like this anymore. I want to live a different way or I don't want to live at all. Please help. I don't want to be a burden. I don't want to ask for prayers. Please remove worry from their minds. Please father. Straighten out everything.
>
> Not another day. I need a change. I need you to overwhelm me with your love. Hold me. Love me. Sit with me and love me.

People who were close to me picked up on the constant anxiety and the depression. But nobody knew what was wrong. I think people just thought I was depressed and frustrated with life. People got mad at my drinking but I don't think they knew it was involuntary. I didn't ask for help. I guess even in blackouts, I stayed tight-lipped. I found out that I would say, "I'm a loser" and talk badly about myself. But I never said, "I have a problem."

I was running most days, I was going to gym, I was attending classes frequently, I was working every day and I rarely called in sick despite throwing up in the bathroom on extra rough days. I ate spinach and hard boiled eggs for breakfast. I ate Paleo for lunch. I occasionally did meal planning when I was functioning well enough. I spent money on manicures and pedicures, I dressed neatly, and I spent time on my makeup. I posted funny things on Facebook, I walked at parks with friends. I took my nieces and nephews out for ice cream and attended their birthday parties. I went to the pool on weekends. Each time I did any healthy activity, I posted pictures on social media. I went to concerts (even though I couldn't tell you which songs played after the beginning), I made appearances at dinners, I worked on craft projects. My captions contained creative ways of saying, "This is my normal life. This is me doing normal things." If I went to a lake or park, you know I was going to document it. Nobody knew that it took all the strength I could muster to appear normal. Every single day was a fight to keep my head above water.

> 10/22/13 I think the most precious gift we glean from mistakes is graciousness toward others. We judge less, we love more. We're all doing our best to our own standards. We all try. Some are weaker, some stronger. But we all give it our best. Our eyes change through every experience. They open wider. We're all searching for peace of mind/happiness. We use whichever road we think will get us there. Some money, success and fame. Others through service and working for the greater good.

Sometimes I would be driving to the gym, and I would just randomly think "fuck it" and I would go pick up a salad and a bottle of wine and go home and drink instead. The intervals of me being sober got shorter and shorter.

Alcohol was consuming me. I felt like I was carrying a big secret. And secrets made me put up walls.

In April of 2014, I had registered to run the Rock N Roll Raleigh inaugural race and I was incredibly underprepared. About a month before the race, I threw my training program to the wind. Most of my weekends were becoming benders, which didn't leave much time for running. My stomach would gurgle and hurt for days. Due to a little WebMD research, I learned that my unmistakable symptoms would've told anyone I had a tear in my intestine or an ulcer in my stomach. Amenorrhea invited itself in. I felt like hell.

My parents came down the day before the race to surprise me. I wasn't prepared for the race. I was in bad shape. I was able to not drink the week before the race. I was scared about my body not being able to handle it because it was hot and humid. I had trouble breathing when I ran two miles the day before the race. I ran my worst race to date (2:03:05). My body was struggling to hold it together. After I crossed the finish line, I told myself I would never run another half marathon. I never wanted to feel this horrible again. Running wasn't fun anymore. So I stopped almost entirely. Fuck that. Fuck humiliating myself. My body can't handle it.

On 4/8/14, the idea for Hopelust was born. I wanted to create a website where people who struggled with various things could share hope and inspirational things. I wanted to create a place where people who were on their lonely islands could communicate so that they would feel less alone. I didn't personally know others who experienced my isolation, loneliness or pain. But I thought an online forum could be anonymous so that way anybody could log in from anywhere and find a sense of hope. The idea didn't make it any further than my journal because I felt as though I didn't have any hope myself, let alone enough to give away.

I decided to join a small personal training gym so that I could get some help managing my weight. I wasn't overweight, but the booze was putting an extra layer on my stomach and I wanted help removing that. I was attending two-a-day boot camps for a while. One at 5 a.m. and another at 6 p.m. For two weeks, I was able to give up alcohol as part of a weight-loss regimen.

When I fell back into the bottle, the shaking got even worse because not only would my hands tremble, my head and face shook and even my voice. It was happening on a regular basis now, during the week, not just on Mondays. I could no longer stand myself. Alcohol started becoming a major limitation; the tether was becoming increasingly shorter. I couldn't schedule an appointment in advance because I didn't know if I would have the shakes that day. I knew I could try not to drink, but I knew that my control was unpredictable so I didn't know if I would be able to abstain from drinking.

My coordination and depth perception were suffering. One Monday morning, I drove my car into the side of the parking garage. I wasn't drunk, though I was disoriented. I was trying to let a car drive beside me and I didn't perceive the space accurately. So my Malibu, lovingly referred to as Freedom because it bucked like a horse due to a transmission issue, had three deep silver grooves on the back passenger side. It became increasingly challenging to keep my car in my lane so I avoided roads with narrow lanes. I had a constant feeling of impending doom. I would drive to work feeling like something horrible was going to happen that day.

My car now looked the part; it matched the driver. It was apparent even to people outside of my car. Now, when I drove to the store to get booze, it looked like I had already consumed some. I needed a new car. I bought an Acura TSX. I no longer looked the part. Now I looked like a young professional who had her shit together. I looked cleaned up. Surely someone who dressed like me and drove my car and looked healthy wouldn't look like she was getting her ass kicked by *it* every day.

I was grateful that I was able to upgrade my car. But I still didn't feel better about myself, I just felt like I was doing a better job of hiding it; I was proud of my ability to blend. I was drinking less for the buzz and more to control the withdrawal from not drinking. My face would turn red and always remained flushed. There were several Mondays where I left work over lunch to drive home to drink a four-ounce measuring cup of wine. I just needed enough to calm down the withdrawal symptoms so that I could function. I had the occasional 5 a.m. four ounce serving of wine to stop the shakes. I never took alcohol to work with me because I didn't trust myself not to drink it.

I would come home from work and show up at my flag football games, all smiles. I would run my heart out, despite the shakes, which were less noticeable when I was moving around. I would go out to eat afterward. I would go to boot camp sessions at my personal training gym. I would outperform the other participants often. I would get healthy eating tips, discuss fasted morning cardio and act like I wasn't carrying a ravenous beast around on my back. Upon leaving wherever I was, I would determine my route home based on which place I would buy wine. Then I would go home and drink myself to sleep. I could drink an entire bottle without feeling drunk if I spaced it out a little. So I had to slam the servings back to back. Otherwise, it wouldn't work.

I continued to participate in life. I would lean against the bathroom vanity and stare in the mirror. I saw my red nose and cheeks; I knew the boozing was enlarging my blood vessels, creating this sun burn colored effect. I saw the dry skin on my face. I saw the wrinkles becoming increasingly apparent; I knew the dehydration from alcohol was magnifying them. I saw my tired, hollow eyes. What was inside? Where was the old Gina? Was she even in there? Drunk Gina was so frail, she was a paper airplane trying to navigate the sky. She wasn't in control of herself. She wasn't strong enough to be okay.

Then I would cry. And cry. And cry. This was my life; my life was in shambles. And I couldn't help myself out of the mess. I was in a raging river full of rapids headed toward a waterfall with a drop off that was going to kill me and I couldn't stop. I didn't have a shore to swim to. I was barely keeping my head above the water to stay afloat. It was dark. And I needed help.

2/17/14 I'm hung over again. I need a hug. I need help. I can't do this alone. God, I need big help. I'm nothing on my own.

I thought *it* only happened to older people. I always pictured the homeless man on the sidewalk with the brown paper bag. I didn't know it happened to people who held down jobs, went to the gym evenings, had families who loved them, had college degrees, were young and healthy and appeared normal otherwise. I didn't know *it* could happen to me. I thought I was somehow invincible and protected from *it*; I didn't know *it* can happen to anyone. I know it sounds naïve and almost arrogant, but I thought people signed up for *it*. Obviously, nobody would choose that.

I used to tell God "Fix this!" or "Take the desire to drink away" or "Make me happy so I stop." And I would yell at Him and say, "Look what You're doing to me! Why won't You give me a reason to stop?" I was angry. So I drank and drank. I thought one day God would show up on a thunder cloud and say, "Gina, you are healed. Your life will now be sunshine and roses and you will live happily ever after!"

Growing up, I had formed the idea that it was possible to avoid pain. I didn't understand that pain was a normal part of life. The pain I felt left me feeling raw and overwhelmed. I looked at people around me and it seemed evident that everyone was happier and doing better than me. Was I broken? Was I damaged and unrepairable? I thought it was just me.

Initially, I thought I could outsmart pain or dodge it. God was going to enable me to do this by providing me wisdom and guiding my steps. I thought if I prayed to Him, I would never experience pain. I thought if I asked Him for something, I would get it right away. To me, He was the easy way around things. That's probably why I prayed to Him. I don't think I actually loved Him or ever trusted Him completely until things got personal. I only began to love Him after it became evident that He actually did love me. In my ugly, dirty filth, He loved me. However, when I looked around at my pain, I assumed I had done something wrong; I assumed that my circumstances were an indication of my worthiness.

I would see other people moving on in life. I felt like God was blessing everyone except me. I saw others getting opportunities that I wanted. When I saw someone get engaged, it felt like a kick in the stomach. It seemed like everyone around me had life happening. They were traveling, getting job offers and starting families. I wasn't. I was still same old Gina being held hostage by alcohol. I felt left behind, unloved, and forgotten.

I knew God existed. Sometimes I knew that He loved me. But I didn't understand why I was still in the pit of hell. I knew He was powerful enough to save me when I called out to Him. He preserved me when I could've been exposed to disease, He protected me during blackouts and He kept me from getting arrested. I knew He was powerful. If He truly loved me, why was I still enduring this hell? How much lower could I sink? How much longer could I last?

Gina Mast
April 13, 2014

Mom and dad drove 9 hours to surprise me for my race. No pressure...

I had the shakes, internal bleeding, amenorrhea, and constant stomach aches. I spent many weekends locked in my apartment, day drinking and passing out whenever. This looks like a happy girl who has loving parents to support her. This alone should have made me happy, but it didn't. I was lucky, I just didn't see it at the time. I saw all the things I didn't have. And I hated life.

CHAPTER 7

Pinot Grigio is the New Coffee Creamer

3/11/14 God I'm mad at you. I'm too young to have such old eyes. Stop my tears. Stop letting me want to die. Stop letting me hate everything about my life. Stop letting it get worse.

2 A.M. INSOMNIA WAS MY lonely hell. I tried not to alert the rest of the world that I was awake because I didn't want anyone to wonder why; I was afraid this would indicate I had an issue. If I had wine around, I would drink a glass to go back to sleep. If I didn't have any, I would walk. I was sweating alcohol. I would shower to get rid of it. But it would be there after I dried off. That smell. I smelled like someone who was dying. I would sit in the shower and cry in the mornings. I couldn't stop shaking. I didn't even feel balanced sitting on the ground. The anxiety was overwhelming. The depression, self-hate, and shame were unbearable.

I might have a good week or two where I wasn't drinking and I would feel so proud of myself and so in control, then a small gust of wind would tip my boat. I would have another drink, and it was as though all the resistance I had built up simply dissolved and I was right back to having the shakes and drinking every single night.

As it progressed, I didn't even want to go anywhere on weekends because I didn't want to try to hide how much alcohol I was consuming. During the day, I tried to hide the shakes. And at night, I tried to hide how much I was drinking. I didn't want to embarrass myself by passing out, so I had more reason to just stay home. I joked about my Sleeping Beauty phase, but I was drinking to the point of passing out. So it became less shameful to just stay home.

I drank wine because it had a higher alcohol content than beer. It was more concentrated and it wasn't carbonated so it was easier to chug, transport, and store. Plus, in North Carolina, they sell it everywhere. I would've had to go to the ABC store to buy liquor. Wine was easier and more affordable. I drank it as a means to an end, not to enjoy it. It was a utility for me.

I kept my wine in my closet. Initially, I kept three identical bottles in the pantry. What my roommate saw was three unopened bottles of wine. What I saw was me emptying the bottles, discarding them when I had insomnia in the middle of the night, and then immediately replacing them so that it looked as though they remained untouched. This worked for a while until I needed to increase the quantity of alcohol I was purchasing. See, only Harris Teeter carried this particular wine. Imagine two-buck chuck, but worse. Well, there were only so many of these stores in my area so I started buying it at other places. It was easier for me to start hiding the bottles in my closet and dresser drawers because they were always different and I wouldn't have been able to hide the amount that I was consuming. Gas stations rarely carry popular brands.

I started buying the gallon jugs. I also bought the small single-serving plastic containers because they were easier to hide. I could keep them in my purse or I could easily duck into my room and chug one during a commercial or during a bathroom break if I had a guest. I could slip a straw into it, tilt it to the side to guzzle it, then stop a few sips short of the empty bubble noises straws make. I could pour the last sip into my mouth and I would be all set. This helped me get rid of the shakes in the morning if I had company. I could quietly return to my peace and minimize the withdrawal symptoms while I had a friend sleeping in the next room, unaware of the girl who was living in Gina's home, drinking early in the morning. At this point, I was judging myself. But I was also applauding myself for surviving and finding ways around obstacles. I could find a way to drink in almost any situation. I realized that I could bury the smell of wine by pouring coffee in with it. I wasn't concerned about taste; I was trying to regain composure. I went to great lengths to hide the bottles when I was ready to take the trash out. All of my efforts went into finding ways to conceal it. I didn't know how to fix it, so I did what I could to work around it.

> Voicemail from Dad 6/9/13: "Gina, this is your dad calling. I just wanted to let you know that you are the most transformed person. You're the best person in America. You're the best person in the world. You are the queen of the Mast family. God is taking you in that direction. I will treat you and look at you as though you were totally perfect already. Have a great day."
>
> (I didn't pick up the phone. It was a Thursday morning. I was ashamed of myself and fearful that he would realize I was a mess. So I avoided him and hid among the 8 other siblings, 17 grandkids, and 6 in-laws). It made me feel guilty when he left voicemails like this. I wasn't leading an honorable life. I was in the bottom of the barrel. I didn't know that one day I would experience transformation. I thought my dad was just trying to encourage me; I didn't know God was speaking to me through him.)

Toward the end of it, I switched to boxes. They held more, and they didn't clink when I threw them in the trash. I kept them in my walk-in closet on a bin that resembled a neat little table. I was clever. I drank Pinot Grigio and I always said I liked the taste of it and the fact that it was lighter. The truth is that my main concern was that it didn't stain. I had been to wine tastings at wineries. Even when I wasn't wasted, I could never pick up on the floral, oaks and citruses that were "embodied" in the wine. Maybe because of my unsophisticated palate or because I drank the cheapest wine I could find, the stuff I drank tasted like shit. I used to put ice in it when I was drinking reds.

But then I realized that if I just chugged it, it went down easier. It's not like the acid was good for my teeth to soak in anyways.

Once on a date, a guy asked me what I liked to do. I had no answer. I felt like a deer in the headlights. What could I tell him? I like to drink. I drink all the time. But I can't tell someone that. What would a normal person be doing if they weren't drinking? I could talk about Paleo eating, meal planning and going to the gym. I could talk about movies or TV shows. I could talk about Netflix or my family. I felt like my brain was dumbing down. I was always distracted. Outside of drinking, my interests were dissolving. I loved to run and paint. But drinking devoured my motivation and ate it all up. I liked to watch movies, but I couldn't even finish them most of the time because I would pass out before the end.

I didn't have much incentive to let people get close to me. The closer they got, the harder it was to hide my drinking. I was hanging out with this guy, Mike. Like when any guy came over, I would sneak my wine when he was in the bathroom. Or I would go into my closet and guzzle some. After spending a bit of time together, he brought up my personality. He didn't understand why sometimes I was so easygoing, lighthearted, and talkative. And the other half of the time I was quiet, pensive, and serious. He didn't like when I was that way. What he was saying is that he didn't enjoy hanging out with me when I was sober. He didn't understand the reason my personality was flopping around.

I would twist open the mini bottles to break the seal in advance, then close them again. I stashed them in my closet, under my bathroom vanity, or under the kitchen sink with a straw folded inside. If I wasn't home, they would be in my car. I could run out to grab my phone charger and emerge minutes later, calmer with the storm inside more under control. This enabled me to reinforce my fortress. If I kept the withdrawals at bay, nobody knew. And if nobody knew, then my secret was safe. I liked having people around, but I loved it when they left. Because only then could I quench the thirst that was badgering me all day. Only then could I stop swimming against the exhausting current. Only then could I find relief.

I eventually learned not to reply to text messages if I had been drinking, unless I was in a blackout because I didn't want to expose myself through incoherent words on a screen. It was easier for me to avoid and ignore than it was to lie. There were unexplainable three to four-hour gaps. I acted like I was busy. But I had been passed out. If someone asked questions, they were prying. And I hated when people pried.

When dating, I tried to avoid situations with alcohol. I would suggest hiking or any outdoor activity. Of course, I was going to drink beforehand, but I didn't want to be able to continue drinking. I tried to manipulate situations to protect myself and others from *it*. When *it* did surface, and *it* always did, I would try to find humor in the chaos. If *it* was mentioned, I danced around the subject. The eyes facing me were often at the intersection of confused and concerned. I would react with an explanation about how much I loved wine and just having fun. Humiliation would fill my body, like a hose filling an aquarium. From my toes, though my legs and torso. I fought it from filling my face. Outside of my fortress, I was stiff with an impenetrable wall. I didn't let you read me; I hated when you looked me in the eyes. Inside, I was crying, I was screaming for help. I wanted you to take your hands and place them on my shoulders. I wanted you to squeeze my arms and reassure me that you will help me out of this. I wanted you to tell me I wasn't alone. But you didn't because you couldn't understand; you probably thought I was still in my college phase. So I was alone.

I wanted help. But I didn't want you to know I needed it. Cause that would've fed my shame. If I was under the gun because I had made a mess during a blackout, I ran. You never stood a chance. I found faults in you before you found out my last name. That way, when I ghosted you, it would be a decision that I made, a situation which was under my control. My choice. When you saw me, I was drunk. So I spaced out hangouts. When I stopped wanting to go out, I realized that if everyone thinks I'm with someone else, no one will know that I'm alone.

When people talk about suicide, they tell you not to do it for your family. People say that suicide is selfish but when you are in that place, it makes you feel like those people are selfish. Because if they knew the pain you felt, they wouldn't ask you to continue suffering through it. At my low point, I felt as though I didn't have the strength from within to rescue myself. How was I going to help anyone else around me? "My family would be better off if I wasn't around. I am a burden. If people really knew me, if they saw into the closet where I hid the contents of my heart, they would be repulsed. If they saw the things I had done, they would throw me out with the trash. I'm worthless. Things will never get better."

I wanted to die. I thought I was running out of options. I didn't know how to do it. I thought I burdened my family and I had myself convinced every single person would be better off without me around. Then Luke committed suicide in May of 2014.

I had worked with Luke's sister at a waitressing job during my first summer after moving to North Carolina, back when I was eighteen. Her and I weren't that close, yet somehow we remained friends on Facebook. I had no idea this small thread of a connection would become a lifeline to me. It was through Facebook that I found out about his death. It turns out, he was just like me. He was only four days older than me. He had fought my same demons and he had been more open about it than me. Even after knowing this, his sister still loved him. She shared his story via social media because she wanted to spread awareness about addiction. She posted truthful things she wished Luke had known. She didn't see him as a burden, she wanted him around more than anything. Somehow, I could imagine my sisters sharing these same feelings with her. This gave me the courage to keep trying; it helped me see that maybe I would hurt people more by abandoning my ship than I would being my messy self. It helped me see that I wasn't alone; I wasn't the only one fighting these demons. She called out the lies he was believing and she spoke truth to them.

 **Gina Mast** added a new photo to the album: **Raleigh By Foot**.
July 31, 2014

I had been up for hours, not because I set my alarm to start the day early with a beautiful sunrise. I had insomnia because I was experiencing withdrawal. I was miserable.

CHAPTER 8

Dreams

I COULDN'T STOP DRINKING. NOTHING worked. I continued having dreams about the future that inspired hope. That lady had said that I was going to have a promising future. I was going to be an honorable person. But she also said the hottie was going to come back. Despite the dreams that followed this storyline, he wasn't there. So maybe it was all empty hope. Having false hope is more devastating than not having hope. Because there is an equal low for the excited anticipation that you feel. So I was bitter with God, with her, with myself, with everyone and with everything.

> 7/3/13 Interesting dreams last night
>
> It was like Dad was in the future. He came back to tell me that I had told him after I met the guy I would spend my life with. I said that the guy was even better than I had imagined he would be. Dad said I was so happy and he wanted me to see how happy I would be.
>
> Lastly, I was in a field surrounded by woods. I was trying to run and hide from ogre giants who were coming after me. They were slow and unskilled killers — but they looked scary. People [angels] were killing them for me. Then a guy [Jesus] let one get close to me. He stood beside me, coaching me how to defeat it. He said, "Stand firmly and you can easily push them over." I

struggled to get my footing and balance. But once I did, I defeated it [the giant represented it.]

Sometimes, I knew that God loved me. But I felt unloved because I hurt every day and every night. I was packing a huge monkey around on my back every day. And then the monkey would beat the shit out of me every single night.

On July 11, 2014, I had a dream. The gentle, comforting voice of Jesus asked me, "Do you want me to heal *it*?" He didn't say what *it* was, but I knew what He meant. I didn't want to label *it*. He didn't label *it* either. There was no judgment in the question. There was warm mercy, grace, and love; it melted my heart. God was watching me, He realized I was in pain and He intended to help me. He was going to heal me.

The gist of the dream was that I had a near death experience involving pythons and Jesus. I was at a resort with my family and I was completing an obstacle course, which I believe represented life. At one point, I had to leave my family to walk down a dirt path to a pond. The last obstacle had to be completed alone, with only the camp leader. I was walking down the muddy path in my bare feet. Suddenly I saw some little pink pythons coming out of the dirt. They were babies. I said out loud, "I should have worn my sandals." And the camp leader told me they would've been useless. Out of the blue, a huge green giant python eyed me down and started coming straight at me. I couldn't outrun it and I was defenseless. I had a few sticks that were the size of straws and wouldn't have been strong enough to puncture the skin of the baby snakes, let alone this monster. I don't know why it targeted me. It didn't seem to be aware of the camp leader. But its sights were set on me and that was that. My heart was pounding as I faced certain death because there was nowhere to run and hide. With the tiny straw in my hands, which were lifted above my head, I called out over and over "Jesus. Jesus. Jesus. Jesus. Jesus." I knew I didn't stand a chance on my own, I knew I was ill-equipped and I needed Him to work a miracle for me. At the last possible second when the snake was right in front of my face, my arms almost involuntarily came down and pierced the head of the snake, killing it. I didn't know this until after it was dead, but this giant python had one tiny area in its skull that could be punctured. Without the knowledge or the skill, through calling out to Him, I overcame it through Him at the last second. Since I was the victor in the dream, I thought this meant that *it* was over.

I had heard of the python spirit before. All I knew was that it was something that wrapped itself around you and attempted to squeeze the life and hope out of you. It let you breathe, then it suffocated you. Then it loosened its grip, then tightened it again. That's how drinking was. It was okay, then it got worse. Then I got hope, then it got worse. I thought the python represented *it* and I thought God would show me I would defeat *it*, like a David and Goliath situation.

I had never noticed the pattern that dreams I had usually showed me events that hadn't happened yet, but would happen in the future. Perhaps so that I call the things as they would be and not as they are? Anyways, when I woke up the next morning, I was crying with joy that I had been healed. I started saying out loud, "I am healed." I was afraid to get near alcohol though. Then, after several days, I randomly felt overwhelmingly lonely, depressed and afraid so I did what I always do: I stopped on my way home and loaded up on alcohol. And I was back at it.

I felt let down and confused. God showed me that I was healed. But it didn't look like it and it certainly didn't feel like it. I would sit on my bathtub floor with the shower water running, sobbing. My legs were too heavy to stand up. I was not going to be able to get through one more day. I couldn't make it one more minute. Even though I didn't see the healing, I kept telling God, "You said I am healed."

 **Joanna Mast** added 2 new photos — with **Gina Mast**.

July 16, 2014 · Raleigh

Zane's bday surprise from Gina. Thank u!

I had the shakes this day. I struggled to hide it under coffee jitters. I often tried to exaggerate enthusiasm, excitement, and jokes to cover how I was feeling inside.

CHAPTER 9

The Dissolution of the Rescue Committee

I DON'T REMEMBER WHERE I heard it first, but I know the Bible says something about the power of life and death lying in the tongue. For most of my life, I thought this was an exaggeration; I thought it was BS. I started feeling the desire to speak life somewhere in 2014, I think. I didn't know sometimes the simple desire to do something is God moving in me. Sometimes He plants the desire in my heart so I feel prompted to do something. He speaks to me so much that I don't even know how to separate it from our own thoughts.

Anyways, I started speaking over my day every morning while I was in the shower. I'm pretty sure it was my sister Katie who shared her routine with me, which I adopted. My brain was a bit foggy toward the end so the specific details are hazy. Anyways, each morning I would say out loud the things God said about me either in the Bible or according to that lady: "I am blessed, I am highly favored, I am deeply loved, I am a child of the most high God, my words have the power to speak life and death and I choose to speak life, I am peaceful, I am whole..." I would ramble on for a few minutes, usually on autopilot. I started adding in that, "I am healed and I am free, I am the head not the tail," etc. Then I spent each night drinking myself into oblivion.

I was completely confused. I felt like I was living someone else's life. I knew that God gave me power over this monster but I couldn't understand why the monster was winning. Why was I the one getting my ass kicked every single day? Why was I drowning when He made me to be victorious? When

I was alone and I was falling apart, I would weep. And I would repeat out loud "You are with me." Because I knew God was with me. Saying it didn't bring about His presence, but it comforted me to know He was near. Because He was always near. He knew the times I screwed up. On the nights when I drank the most, He would give me a sweet dream that inspired hope. When I deserved it the least, He showed His love the most. So I knew He was always there.

Since the drinking continued and the healing wasn't apparent, I had lost all hope. I just wanted to die. I would hear the lies: a) I am not strong enough, b) I cannot do this, c) nobody wants me here, d) everyone would be better off if I was just gone, d) I'm an embarrassment to my family, e) everyone has given up on me, f) I have nothing to live for, g) I'm worthless, h) all hope is gone, etc. It was at this time that I would think of Luke. I remembered the things that his sister had posted after his suicide. The light from the truth she spoke would confront my darkness. The lies I heard would wrestle with this truth, and somehow the truth was enough to give me the courage to go one more day. Always just one more day.

My sister from Florida texted me on 7/20/14. She knew less about my drinking than anyone. I saw her maybe twice a year and we didn't talk much in between. She said that God wanted me to know that what looks like my death will be my miracle and that God would part my sea for me. She said to get ready for my story. I think we all thought that God was talking about stopping the hottie from getting married, because at this point he had gotten engaged. I had shared the dreams openly with my sisters. It was one of the few good things I had that I could talk about. Secretly, I thought that he was going to come back and save me. I thought that *it* would take care of itself when he came back. But this hope wavered. Sometimes it felt close and I had zero doubt that the story could turn out any other way. Sometimes it felt like a vapor of smoke. When it felt like a joke, I doubted that God would heal me.

But God wasn't talking about the hottie showing up. God was talking about *it*. He was talking about my rescue from *it*. At this time, I didn't see it though. What did I see? My rescue committee was planning on getting married. And I saw *it* continue to dominate and rule my life. Where was God in this? Was He going to show up? He said I was healed, but it didn't look like it. And it didn't feel like it.

On 8/7/14 I had a dream. I was in a huge warehouse with God. The entire warehouse was full of those gas station refrigerators. You know the kind with the glass doors where you can see what's inside? The ones that hold the sodas? Well, God said to me, "I know you're hungry. I know you haven't eaten in two years. You can eat anything you want to." I was excited. I ran around the warehouse, looking from door to door. Then I did something that wasn't like my younger self. I didn't touch any of the contents. I came back over to God and asked Him what I should eat. I knew that I could have anything that I wanted but I didn't want to do it my way. My way was broken; I knew I wouldn't make good decisions on my own. I wanted to seek His wisdom on doing things the best way. I was starving for love, hope and life. I wanted His love and I wanted freedom. My life had been in the pit of hell for two years, and I was ready to come up for air. Desperation gave me the desire to seek God's will on matters.

On 8/30/14, the remainder of my hope was extinguished. The rescue crew that my dreams had painted wasn't going to come for me. When the hottie got married, I finally gave up on waiting for him to come save me. I thought maybe my alcohol brain had been damaged. Did God allow me to have a sense of false hope to give me something to look forward to so that I have a reason to keep holding on? Even though the dreams were vividly detailed and the things the lady said checked out, I felt stupid. I felt I'd been led astray by God. Why had I spent years waiting for someone to show up when they weren't coming? I was mad God let me walk down a bunny trail in the wrong direction for years without correcting my path. If He didn't stop me from walking in the wrong direction, if He didn't keep the hottie for me like the dreams indicated He would, why then would He rescue me from the drinking? The hottie wasn't coming, and God wasn't coming through. Who was going to save me? I was on my own.

I didn't have a reason to hope. I didn't see a reason to live. My heart was beating but I was dead inside. I wanted to feel something. I'm not sure where the idea came from but I bought a Groupon to go skydiving. If fear was what I would feel, I didn't care. I just wanted to feel alive. I was afraid, but I honestly didn't care if I survived. Skydiving wasn't so much courage as it was not caring if the parachute strings snapped and I free-fell into the ground. Dying would've ended my misery. And if I lived, then I might actually feel something.

I felt a rush of excitement and fear. I got home around 2 p.m. on a Saturday. I was nervous about telling my mom I had gone skydiving, so I needed to drink so that I could tell her. Plus it was a long afternoon, what could I do to occupy myself until my friend's birthday dinner around 7 p.m.? I had offered to be the designated driver to prevent myself from getting too drunk. But then when I got home, I didn't stop drinking until I passed out. I woke up hours later with a million missed calls and text messages. I showed up at the birthday party downtown. I had driven there and managed to forget my ID and money. I had to Uber home to get it. Then my other friend ended up putting me in a cab during a blackout. I woke up in a cab with the driver asking me where I was going. Apparently, she didn't give him the correct address or something. He could have killed me. Anything could have happened. Anyways, the excitement I had felt didn't last. Nothing ever lasted. I was damned to live in this fucking hell. Fuck life. Fuck everything about life.

I was angry. I had been forsaken and left behind. I had been abandoned, overlooked and forgotten. If I was blessed, why didn't it look like it? If I was the "head and not the tail," why the fuck did it feel like I was losing? I didn't know why God was allowing this. Why wasn't He saving me? I would see other people financially prospering and talking about how good God was. I wasn't asking Him for success. I mean I was, but I was trying to get my head above water first. I just wanted to get back to zero. I just wanted to be okay. God was blessing literally every other person except me. Was I doomed to spend my life lonely; trapped inside a miserable hell? Aside from the dream about me being healed, He never gave me a dream that showed that I would, in fact, be free because *it* never blatantly came up in the dreams. So I didn't know. Maybe this would be my lot in life. I knew there were things about God that I didn't understand. Maybe this was one of those things.

It was dark, it was cold and it was barren. I was wasting away inside and out. I didn't want to feel another minute of it. I didn't want to keep breathing. I just wanted to stop waking up. I was just too tired to keep trying to swim. I was broken, my bones felt heavy. I was weak and fatigued. Trudging through life was more than I could bear; I wasn't fucking strong enough. I couldn't do this. If this was what life was, I didn't fucking want it. Fuck that. That was fucking hell.

Sometimes it was easier to just avoid people. Fuck trying to pretend to be okay. Fuck trying to look happy. I felt so frail and fragile; I couldn't keep trying to hold it together. My muscles felt like they were deteriorating. My heart was empty of anything good. I didn't feel love, joy, or peace. I felt hatred, anger, abandonment, loneliness, shame, and pain. There was so much damn pain. It hurt all the time. I cried most days. Sometimes if I held it together for the day, I would get home to my apartment building. And sometimes I couldn't even make it to my front door before the tears started pouring out.

I would try to buy booze in advance. I hated when the cashier saw I had been crying. Cause it's sad when you sell alcohol to a sad person. You can't look sad or depressed when you're buying it. Cause then they will know you are self-medicating. You have to buy it when you're in good shape; you have to be cleaned up. You have to act happy. You have to act like it's for the pool or for a dinner. There was so much pretending. Nothing felt real. Nothing except the agony that I carried every day, like a heavy cloak. My insides were a sludgy wasteland of decomposing organs. My gurgling stomach reminded me of it regularly. And the stomach aches fucking hurt. You know what would sometimes dull them? More booze. Cause I couldn't wait for them to go away. Sometimes it would take like three days after a bender weekend. Sometimes a full week.

It's almost like I didn't want to live until I felt like the choice was being taken away from me. I didn't know why I was getting random nosebleeds, I only knew I was getting them. I would try to hide them because I was afraid it was a tell-tale sign of my drinking. I didn't know why there was evidence of internal bleeding; I still don't know if it was an ulcer or a ruptured intestine. I used Google to research alcohol abuse and when I read stuff that scared me, I would stop. I was overflowing with fear. I knew that if I kept drinking, I would die. Whether it be from eventually and unknowingly driving in a blackout, getting killed during a blackout downtown, or rotting to death. But I knew I was going to die. I had done the research and watched documentaries. I knew what happened to people eventually. And I knew that I was doomed.

My rock bottom wasn't one big pivotal moment. I didn't end up in jail or the hospital. I think I finally realized that nobody was going to come save me. I knew that I was going to have to try to save myself or I would die for real. I knew it was going to be a slow and painful death. And the thought of enduring the suffocation wasn't something I was going to be able to bear. It wasn't black and white, it was a gray area. I think it was losing all hope in an external force coming to save me.

Without a reason to hope, without a reason to think a rescue committee was on the way, without my health, without an explainable reason, I started wanting to get help and quit. I didn't really trust God one hundred percent. He had said I was healed but I wasn't seeing it. I wasn't sure if my words really did have power, but if they did, I continued to speak life each day because that was something I could do without God's assistance. I had zero faith that I would get sober. I didn't believe in myself. But with my body falling apart and knowing that I was going to lose the choice to live, I decided to try to become healthier; I was resigned to the fact that I would always drink.

Gina Mast updated her profile picture.
September 21, 2014

'Cause I'm on top of the world, 'ay
I'm on top of the world, 'ay
Waiting on this for a while now
Paying my dues to the dirt
I've been waiting to smile, 'ay
Been holding it in for a while, 'ay
Take you with me if I can... See More

The only thing that made this caption true was the fact that I was literally on top of the world, due to skydiving. I didn't care if I survived the jump because I thought I had nothing to live for.

CHAPTER 10

Clarity

I REMEMBER LAYING IN MY bed early in the morning on September 27, 2014 sobbing. I had sent a birthday message to my ex from 2011's sister. It made me reflect on the life I used to have and made me wonder what had become of me. Where did I go wrong? How did I get here? My life was in shambles. I had nothing to show for myself. I was a fucking joke. Obviously, I started drinking because I was awake. And when I started drinking, I didn't stop. That vacuum pulled me into that first drink because I needed it to function. I needed it to breathe. I needed it just to be okay. Once I had it, I would be fine. Only that wasn't enough. It was never enough. It was in this "gray" area on this particular morning that I realized there was something wrong. I know, it's a wonder how I graduated from college with such awful reasoning skills.

Anyways, once I got on the slippery slope of a blackout, I wanted help. I didn't want to go into the blackout anymore. I wanted to call my sister and ask for help, I wanted to ask her why it happened every time. But I knew she wouldn't know. I knew she couldn't help me. One thing finally clicked though: one drink put me on the slippery slope into a blackout, every time. One drink removed any willpower and discipline. One drink removed any fucks that I had to give.

But I didn't know how to stay away from that first drink. It was 7 a.m. on a Saturday, I was 25 years old, what some people consider pretty, and aside from *it*, I was healthy, yet I didn't want to do a damn thing. I was lying in bed, crying. And I just wanted to drink myself to sleep. I had no interest in going for a run like I used to. I had no interest in going to the pool. I just wanted to pass the fuck out and get away from myself. I didn't want to look around at the prison that had consumed me. I didn't want to feel anything. I just wanted to sleep. So that's what I did. I drank myself to sleep. I wanted to do better but I didn't know how to change. The weekend glossed over like many of the weekends before it.

Gina Mast
September 26, 2014

I like to think that in heaven: 1) every day is a Friday, 2) there are no school buses to get stuck behind, 3) fingers don't break, and 4) food has zero calories.

> I had heaven on my mind because I wanted to die. I would post funny things to distract from how depressed I was. I had to leave work over lunch to get a box of wine because the shakes were starting to get bad and I knew they would only escalate if I waited until after work.

CHAPTER 11
Drip-Dry

I can't tell you how many declarations I made in my journal promising never to drink again. I had set so many challenges and I had failed at every single one. This last time was different. Since I didn't have hope that I could eliminate alcohol, I set a new challenge on Monday 9/29/14: every day I would make a list in my journal about the things I had done that day that would lead to a better tomorrow. I couldn't force out the old habits but I could allow in the new. Instead of trying to chase out the darkness, I allowed some light in.

Instead of my typical bullshit, "I'm not going to drink" journal entry, I took a gentle approach. The items on my list felt like drops in the ocean, but I felt gratitude for every single drop. I was desperate to feel better. I hadn't felt gratitude in a long time, but I felt gratitude for these small things.

I didn't sleep at all that first night. This was becoming common on Monday nights after a bender weekend. My body was experiencing withdrawal so I had insomnia. Netflix got me through it. I didn't want other people to know I was awake so I would stay off social media and behave like a hermit. The sweats were annoying. Sometimes I would sweat so much that it looked as though I had wet the bed. I hadn't wet the bed. I was just sweating like crazy.

After my flag football game on 9/29/14, I went out and got four mini bottles of wine; the single serving containers. I was trying to taper off because the withdrawal was hell. I drank the bottles as slowly and as spaced apart as I could. I aimed to squeeze in a few hours between each bottle. I wasn't even buzzed a tiny bit. It took about two bottles for the shaking to calm down a little. I took a serving of Nyquil around 8 p.m., hoping I would go to sleep early and avoid the discomfort my body was experiencing. But I didn't. I didn't close my eyes that night. I didn't sleep for a minute.

> 9/30/14 What did I do today to set myself up for a happier tomorrow?
> 1) Fasted cardio (30 minutes)
> 2) Ate paleo breakfast
> 3) Only had 1 coffee
> 4) Drank water
> 5) Spoke truth

It was September 30th. I couldn't tell you if it was actually warm outside or if my body was just perspiring from withdrawal. But I was sweating. My playlist consisted of two songs that I played on repeat: Mercy Me's *Greater* and NeedToBreathe's *Multiplied*. That was the one thing that brought a small sense of peace: knowing Jesus was with me and that He wasn't judging me, He was loving me out of this mess. I felt swallowed up in His love. He loved me through the lyrics. He became my rescue committee; He was my rescuer. He showed up. Every minute. He was inside my bones and inside my muscle fibers. He anchored me and gave my limbs the strength to keep going, one foot in front of the other. We did it in baby steps.

    The same thing happened the next night, which was my first actual night of sobriety because I didn't ease the shakes with any booze. I had a stomach ache, the shakes, and anxiety, but I didn't drink. I had sweats and I was exhausted, but I didn't drink. My body smelled like a dead person and my insides still gurgled like a wasteland, but I didn't drink. My eyes blinked during every minute again. Part of me felt like I would go insane from being so tired, yet part of me felt such pride and strength in not caving and not picking up a drink. I knew that I could alleviate every withdrawal symptom immediately by running to the gas station less than a mile from my apartment. But I also knew that if I did, the withdrawal would be waiting for me the next night. So I lay awake all night, reading subtitles to a show about a serial killer, trying to compose myself. The lead character in the show, Dexter, kept me company. I had anxiety but I saw the tiniest ray of hope and held onto a strand of perseverance. I don't know if I talked to Jesus that night. I probably reminded myself He was with me, but I don't think I could've carried a coherent conversation.

I hadn't slept in 48 hours. On day two (10/1/14) of actual sobriety, my list included:

> 1) Ate healthy breakfast smoothie
> 2) Got a book idea (kinda)
> 3) Spoke life
> 4) Got shitload of supplements at health food store; wanna restore body
> 5) I slept about five to six hours.
>
> I'm still shaking all day and all night. Having an entire 24 hour period without alcohol gives me a little hope. Maybe I'll aim for 100 days of sobriety. I wanna journal how my life changes. Tidbits, experiences, turning points. About recovery and healing and extending grace to ourselves. Humor and hope and healing.

Initially, I wanted to last for 100 days. Then I went back and changed it to a year. The weird thing is that I wasn't that tired. I was out of it, but I was physically functional. The anxiety from the withdrawal almost fueled me. When it was a reasonable hour to get up, like 4 a.m., I went out walking. I walked and walked and walked. I could smell the wine in my sweat, along with the smell of death oozing out of my pores. My sweat betrayed me; it was releasing my secret out into the open. I could smell the wasteland leaking out in the droplets that were seeping out of my skin.

> Day 3 10/2/14 Holy fuck, I feel tired. I hope it's from the calming supplements. But fuck.
> 1) Morning Cardio; jogged part instead of walking. Ran 3 miles. It didn't feel like it was that far

2) Made healthy breakfast
3) Took supplements
4) Had coffee in place of Diet Coke
5) Spoke life

Had another nightmare last night. Developed a fever (I have had chills).

Skydiving was a reset. No. I feel like in order to be happy, one must grow. Always. Do shit that scares you (even if it's just going out to eat). Plan stuff. Try stuff. Write a book or poetry. Cook a new dish. Just keep growing. When you're stagnant, the walls close in.

Note: today's challenge was eating alone. Of course I wanted to blend in. As luck would have it, I choked on salad. I coughed and made everyone look.

I don't know if I was hallucinating, but I thought my closet smelled like wine. And I could smell it in my bedroom and my bathroom. My side of the apartment must have wreaked from it. One night, shortly after I stopped drinking, the smell of the wine that had dribbled on the closet carpeting was overwhelming me. So during my withdrawals, I decided it was a bright idea to bleach the carpet surrounding the space where I'd been keeping my boxes of wine. Soap wasn't enough to get rid of the spot. I was desperate to completely remove this smell. It was a reminder of my guilt and shame. I was having nightmares and seeing ghosts. I thought there was a small child ghost in my room. It hadn't occurred to me that one might hallucinate when experiencing withdrawal. I was familiar with the shakes, cold sweats, blushing, and a shaking voice. But these were new.

Day 4 Friday 10/3/14

I feel happy, albeit tired. So unbelievably tired. I don't understand. Another nightmare last night. So exhausted. I slept through fasted cardio. I assumed my body needed the rest. It must be fighting hard to bounce back.

It wasn't this hard back in April when I quit for 2 weeks to lose weight. What's the difference? I was working out way more and eating cleaner. I had just ran a half marathon.

I'm ultra-fatigued. My mood is improving.

Be free. Be free. And gracious and kind and free.

Be patient Gina. Be good to your body. You are stopping now. Be calm. Wait It'll get better. Hug yourself. You're a champ. You're doing great.

I ordered a Tiffany bracelet with a dove. To wear every day. $150. I want a daily reminder this year of who I am and of hope, peace, and freedom. So pumped.

The average bottle of wine was $7.50. 1 a day (being conservative) is $2,737.50. Holy fuck (That's not including bar tabs, cab rides, Uber charges, late night pizza deliveries, etc. That's just the alcohol I drank in secret).

More focused at work. Longer attention span. Slightly less anxious.

The highlight of the night was that we went to Emma's for family night. I was chill, not anxious. I volunteered to drive Cam so they could drink. I felt responsible & important & useful & involved.

Day 5 Saturday 10/4/14

Three nightmares last night. Ran first thing when I got up. Felt hung over. 4 miles is farther than I've ran in a long while. I ran errands then cleaned the house from top to bottom. I bought fall décor. On the way to dinner at Josis, I felt free. Like I did when I was young. It's the best feeling. I was glad she invited me because I was running out of stuff to clean and was getting antsy.

I drank a ton of diet soda. I had one in hand all day to get my fix. I was carefree and silly at dinner. I felt like my younger self. I felt connected with everyone and drove home after the movie and it's late. I've been eating more. I think I snack and drink diet soda to fill the void of always having a drink in hand. I made a wreath before dinner. For Halloween. A new kind. I felt creative. I'm inspired to paint. I got Joe to help assemble my easel. I'm still kind of shaky. But I think it's from caffeine. Oh and I've been breathing very heavily.

On Thursday, I was praying around 3:30 at work. I was staring out the office window at the bright blue sky. And I finally asked God about the hottie. I hadn't talked to Him about it since the wedding. It was such a sore spot. You know when a wound is ripped open, you don't want to wipe it with an abrasive until some scar tissue builds up? Well, that's how my heart felt. It felt like it was raw and bloody. I can't describe the abandonment I felt. But it hurt like hell. Especially because I wrongfully believed He would save me from it. It wouldn't have been so bad if I hadn't thought I heard God and that He was leading me, guiding me and preserving me. After seeing that lady a short while after our initial meeting, she told me that I shouldn't be mad at God because He was going to keep this guy for me; He wasn't keeping him from me. So all of me believed that God was going to pull out a wild card at the last second and come through. I felt shocked. It hurt down into my ribs. The panic I felt leading up to the wedding was agonizing. Then it happened. My worst fear of being misled happened. Because he got married. I think I was tired of throwing my hissy fit and I finally gained the courage to calm down and talk to God about it. I dared to venture into the place of hurt because I wanted to make peace with it and find healing.] I asked God how I can know my dreams have merit and that I hear His voice. [I thought that I must have misunderstood this situation and I wanted to know how I could prevent it from happening again. How could I protect myself from this feeling of confusion, rage and pain? How could I advise my future children about things if I couldn't even figure out how to navigate life myself? I didn't hear anything apart from silence. I felt peaceful but that was all.] Less than 5 minutes later, the hottie showed up downstairs. [This was strange because my office wasn't in a busy part of town, it's in North Raleigh. I never found out what he was doing there. He just randomly showed up.]

Day 6 Sunday 10/5/14

Tired and don't feel like writing. Woke up around 9. Ran errands and Eva came along. Came home and did laundry. Went to Body Pump with Eva. Went to Fresh on Glenwood for ice cream. Came home. Annie made dinner for us (Shepard's pie). We watched some Netflix then I worked on a pumpkin acrylic painting. I felt mostly restless and homesick and melancholy and lonely. I'm actually excited about this week to see how much better I feel. So I'm way more productive sober.

More bad dreams last night. Craving a feel good something but not alcohol. Sunday nights suck. I will find a way to enjoy them. Maybe art night? IDK. God, spend Sunday nights with me? I'm so glad I'm sober. God, father, Heavenly Father, THANK YOU!

On day #8, I wanted to feel less alone. I couldn't openly discuss the withdrawal symptoms I was experiencing. It was apparent that I wasn't drinking because nobody who knew me could miss the fact that I didn't have a glass of wine attached to my hand.

It was hard to carry this secret alone. I was so proud of every day I was getting of sobriety but I felt like I had nobody to share this excitement with because nobody else fought this exact battle before. I felt like I needed to relearn how to live without alcohol. I was looking for a sense of community. I wanted to find a way to occupy my Sunday nights. I didn't know if I wanted to attend a support group. I would have asked advice from my family, but I didn't think they would understand. I also thought that they would be embarrassed of me. I knew that I wanted and needed to do this myself. This was one of the first times in my life where I had to rely on myself to make a decision. Nobody around me had stood where I was standing and I had to choose for myself. This was when I started learning to rely on God. Because only He knew what was best for me. I knew that everyone else was just going through life, doing the best they knew. I knew that my decisions hadn't really worked out. So I started asking God to call the shots for me. I wanted Him to drive the wheel of my car. He doesn't do that, but He gives us road signs.

I was feeling free and unlimited. I felt like the world was opening up; it was huge and full of opportunities. So on a Tuesday, I looked up a women's support group. I just wanted to be around women who understood me.

> 10/5/14 Wow, I feel hugged all over. Nothing is better than being in a room surrounded by people who understand you, who have felt your pain, shame, and guilt. There were mothers, grandmothers, single women and married women. There were girls my age. Girls who ran. Girls just like me. There were so many warm eyes and smiles and words.

The next day, I told two of my sisters about my experience. Their reactions meant a lot: they were both accepting and understanding.

The next few weeks were a roller coaster of emotions. I had trouble focusing, my mind felt like it had a tornado inside of it. I knew that research shows that in less than two weeks, some brain reversing occurs and that I should be able to tell a difference, so I was feeling hopeful this would change. I used food to cope with the restlessness. I experienced a lot of frustration and irritability. I felt uptight because for years I had used alcohol to help me open up. Without it, I had to build up the courage to open up. This was a slow and painful process. Sometimes this discomfort made me want wine. It was like my bedtime blanket and it was gone now. So I ate ice cream instead.

I hated Sundays, particularly in the fall. Fall is like a Sunday. It's hard to enjoy it because you know that winter/Monday is going to come next. I didn't know how I was going to handle this because my comfort was gone. Food was an alternative, but it didn't do the trick like alcohol. It helped enough. I sought peace and desired to feel loved. Instead of pursuing a relationship for a distraction, I sought God's love. I wanted Him to help me feel less lonely.

For the first time in my life, on Day #13, I noticed a verse in the Bible. 1Peter 5:8 "Be sober, be vigilant; because your adversary the devil, as a roaring lion, walketh about seeking whom he may devour." So many awful things happened that it was hard to imagine working through it all. I wanted to tell people about my choice so that they might forgive my actions, plus I was proud of myself. But after my track record, I didn't think people would believe me.

My emotional spectrum was increasing by the day. The loneliness I had been running from for years was almost breathtaking. It had been waiting there for me. Since I had avoided it so much, it had a lot of catching up to do. I had to process these real feelings. I had to be okay with this loneliness. It felt like I had woken up outside, in the middle of winter, without a jacket or any warm clothing. The cold stung my bare skin; I was unprepared. Since my coping skill was limited to drinking, I had to develop new ones.

After two weeks, I knew I needed to start eating less and I needed to stop trying to numb out the feelings. I found quotes on Pinterest I identified with "When you think you can't, you better fucking convince yourself you can and push harder" and "I tried to drown my sorrows in alcohol but the bastards learned how to swim," by Frida Kahlo. I was running every morning. I decided to get a haircut and start tanning so that I would have a little instant gratification in my journey to getting my health back.

I was waking up around 4 a.m. to do morning workouts again. I considered finding a new job and I had a job offer on the table, but I wasn't sure what I wanted to do. I wanted to sell all my belongings and backpack across Europe. I wanted to experience adventure; I had lost time to account for. I was in a place of extreme transition so I sat tight and told God that I want His best for me; I wanted Him to lead me. On day #17, I was feeling angry and tired. I was getting glimpses of the way my life could have been. But I didn't want to regret it because it made me into the kind hearted person who I had become.

10/16/2014 You were learning. And learn you did. Sweet child, your best days are up ahead.

Facing family dynamics when I was sober was tough. I felt insignificant, sad and bored. I struggled with feelings of insignificance in general; I felt like I didn't matter. I was homesick for a home that didn't exist. I think I was homesick for alcohol. It would've filled the void. But instead, I had to sit in the void. I asked God to step into this void with me and be the fatherly figure that I had long desired. I wanted Him to become my home, my security, my comforter. On day #23, I liked myself for the first time that I can remember. I liked who I was and I liked who I was becoming. Not drinking at social events was hard but it slowly became easier.

A girl I met at the women's meeting, who would eventually become my mentor in the support group, invited me to attend her regular co-ed meeting. I started going there for something to do. I went to meetings during times when I was lonely. But still, I didn't want to fill the lonely void with food or meetings or things, I wanted to feel okay in the void.

On day #34 11/4/14, I didn't miss wine on a Sunday. I wasn't very restless or lonely; peace was beginning to seep into my life. There were waves of bitterness and confusion. The gratitude I had for my health helped me deal with the emptiness I was feeling. I would ask God to meet me today and to just show up to me. I asked Him to help me forgive others when the bitter feelings would arise. I had done things in blackouts that upset people; so when people were mean, I had zero awareness of why. So I struggled with feeling bitter to what I deemed cruelty. So I had to ask God to do the forgiving for me or to help me see things the way He saw them.

I continued to exercise and work on my health. I had weighed as much as I had my freshman year of college. I realized I'd given myself enough time to adjust and I really wanted to start getting disciplined with my diet and nutrition. On good days, it was easier. On bad days, it wasn't. I wanted to ease the blow of sobriety but I didn't want to replace it with another buffer. I didn't want to become reliant on food for comfort, the way I had relied on alcohol. Otherwise, I would fall from one pit into another.

On day #44 11/12/14 I felt an identity crisis. I had been the partier, the boozer. I had been fun, messy, loud, pretty and drunk. Who was I? I felt boring, nerdy, strange, and in control. Knowing that I'll always be in control felt foreign. I liked the stability, but part of it felt scary. I knew that I would have to own all of my actions and I was scared about having to be responsible for my choices because I wasn't sure if I would make poor choices. Most of my decisions when I was drinking were horrible. But I could always say "I was drunk" because I was always drunk. I knew that from here on out, I couldn't point to alcohol. I was going to have to point to myself and accept blame if I goofed up. This was intimidating.

It was also intimidating to face people without a buffer. It was unnerving to show my face in circles where I had disgraced myself during my drinking days. I wanted to tell everyone, "Hey! I'm not drinking anymore. Look at my life, I'm getting it together!" But I didn't because I didn't want people to know that my drinking was so bad that I had to stop entirely. I also didn't want people to treat me differently or treat me like I was fragile, so I made up excuses. "I'm training for a half marathon." "I'm trying to lose weight." "I'm driving tonight." "I have to get up early tomorrow." My family knew that I stopped but I tried to limit how many others knew that I had quit for good. Because I wanted people to act normally. Drink if you drink, don't if you don't. I wanted to be treated as though I were normal. It made me comfortable when other people were comfortable. It stressed me out if I felt like I was inconveniencing someone or making them feel like they couldn't drink simply because I wasn't drinking. Back when I was drinking, I hated people who didn't drink because they made me uncomfortable. I didn't want to be that to other people.

> 7/13/16 Oftentimes, we are unaware of our ability to do something until it has been done. Whatever challenge you're up against, know that you can handle it. You are strong enough. You are tough enough. You were designed to persevere, conquer, and overcome. You are made of grit. You have everything you need from within.

Alcohol gave me courage. Without it, I had to show up anyways. I knew that even if I had a megaphone, I could tell people I was making better choices but I would be unable to change their opinion of me or change their judgment of me. I was unable to go back in time and remove the photographic memories of me making a fool of myself.

> 2/9/15 I always love running because I usually have some of my biggest epiphanies while running. On Saturday it hit me: I constantly try to avoid judgment. When I was drinking, I was concerned about people judging me. I thought it would all go away if I stopped drinking. But it hasn't. Because now people judge me for not drinking. When you have peace and you feel peaceful, the chaos in the world doesn't get you caught up in turbulence. When you follow your peace, you can fall asleep at night knowing you took care of your stuff. When you follow your peace, you don't care as much when people judge you, their judgment doesn't weigh on you. And when you feel peaceful with your decisions, you give others the freedom to make their decisions. If I feel peaceful about not drinking, I should stay peaceful when others drink.

Accepting that I was unable to change the way others viewed me was hard; but letting go of this desire lightened my load. All I could do was quietly show up, stone cold sober, with sweaty hands and trembling legs, with fear, shame, pain, and guilt. I could show up, in spite of these things, and I could be kind. I could not do anything to change the things I had done, I could only change the things I was going to do today. I could only start living differently and leave a different impression moving forward.

Even then, I knew that everyone wouldn't like me. If being awkward was a desirable skill, I would have a strong resume. I'm socially awkward and shy. I hate small talk. I'm kind but I'm shy so sometimes I make others uncomfortable. But that's who I am. God makes no mistakes, He designed me to be this way, quirks and all. If I love myself and can be gentle with myself, while striving to become a better person each day, then that's enough. I am enough, exactly as I am. We all are.

I had to accept that even Sober Gina is going to rub some people the wrong way. When that happened, and it still happens today, I have had to make the decision to let it go. I often imagine a great big canyon. I cup my hands and let all of the fears, expectations and judgments collect. Then I open my hands and let the wind scatter them away. I ask Jesus to help me let them go. When I keep my palms open and stop hanging onto them, they do leave. I can give it to God and ask Him to show them my heart and my intentions. But I cannot make them like me. And that's okay. Caring about others' opinions weighed me down. I became more carefree when I realized I could let it go. Sometimes I catch myself caring. The fear of judgment sneaks up from behind and catches a piggyback ride around on my shoulders. Sometimes the knots in my shoulders give me the awareness of it. Then I have to re-release this fear to get rid of the weight and remind myself to let it go.

Waves of anger arose, followed by waves of forgiveness. Life episodes which had long ago been concluded were resurfacing and finding new conclusions. When those around me started feeling used to me being sober, they resumed their drinking. At times this felt isolating. When I felt grumpy or boring or alone, I would go home early. Because that was better than staying, drinking and being a miserable disaster.

On day #48 11/16/14, I realized I stopped hating Sundays. I didn't fear them and they didn't overwhelm me because I knew how to navigate the loneliness a little better. My mood was improving since I wasn't constantly exposing my body to a depressant. The coping skills I had developed were working and the peace continued to drip into my story.

> Today is day #113. I remember how huge 2 weeks was. And then 30 days felt like I earned a medal. 60 days was a trophy. 90 days was a new car. And now I'm already at #113. I'm excited that the days blend more and more, in that regard. Because now it's less foreign and more regular to be sober at events. I have new habits and new routines. So it feels like regular life instead of like I'm missing part. That was the hardest thing after detoxing. I felt like life had a big hole in it. Sunday nights aren't lonely nights I'm afraid of. They are now one of my favorite nights to relax and unwind before the week. I am looking forward to a full year under my belt. The worst part now isn't fear of life. And it isn't loneliness or anxiety. It's memories.

> Thursday 1/22/15 The more time that passes, the more I see the good from the painful experience of drowning in alcohol. One of my favorite quotes is something like "rock bottom is the solid foundation on which I built my life." And something like "not until we are lost do we find ourselves." Without winter, we couldn't fully appreciate summer. There is another quote along the lines of "constant sunshine creates deserts" or something like that. Seasons make trees blossom! In the winter, trees look dead, dead, dead. There isn't anything left in them and we should lose hope in them ever getting new flowers and growing. But it's the growing season for the roots! It's alive inside, though it doesn't look it. It's growing! And it's preparing to hold more blossoms than it did the year before! How exciting is that? Life's

winters ground us! And strengthen us! How lucky are we? Every winter makes us stronger. And every spring is more beautiful than the one before. So we should be excited when we hit a winter, because that means we're the closest to spring. We're the closest to fresh life and new beginnings! And, we have a story to tell. So that the next person who is in life's winter realizes spring is coming! We know the seasons. When it's winter, we tough it out with the expectation that spring will arrive. Well life happens. And when we get through our winter, we can assure the next person that the season passes. And it gets better. It would be nice if this could be done without gaining additional wrinkles. Trees gain rings in their trunks. I gain wrinkles on my face. We should be proud of wrinkles. They tell stories of triumph and hope! They show we have weathered life's storms and we're here to talk about it. Society makes us want to hide and erase wrinkles. The same way they want us to hide freckles and crooked teeth. I want to change that. Maybe not on a huge scale. But I can impact those in my circle through life. Because even if I don't say it, if I live it, people will feel it.

I don't think I could've remained sober that first year without the help from the support group. Working through a twelve step program helped me learn how to live again. I developed coping strategies. I increased the time I spent journaling. I confronted feelings, sorted them out, and got to the root of my problems. I accepted responsibility for my past mistakes and issued apologies I had owed others. I stopped seeing myself as just a hostage victim; I started to see my part in things. I learned not to carry the stress or negativity of others. I took care of my business, then left others' business alone. I stopped pretending and I stopped hiding from myself and others. I acknowledged my flaws and granted myself permission to have them. I worked through all the emotions I'd been resisting for so long. It was an emotional cleansing

I have had to forgive myself. I put up two wallet sized pics on my bathroom mirror. Aged 5 & 15. I try to talk to myself like I would talk to the 5 year old Gina. All I see is her sweet eyes and her cuteness. She was adorable. She was too young to know which clothes were cool. She wasn't comparing herself to others. She loved and she was loved. She made people smile. I always thought I was an ugly duckling growing up. I can't go back and encourage that Gina, but I consider her when I get ready for the day. I want to see myself through those eyes. So that I don't regret it when I'm 90. I don't want to point out my flaws to myself anymore. I want to recognize the things that make me authentic and different, and learn to adore those things.

15 year old Gina was full of fire and ready to conquer the world. She wasn't jaded, she saw possibilities. Though she didn't love herself like 5 year old Gina, she wasn't ashamed of herself. She wasn't a failure and she didn't let people down.

I don't want to let my life with alcohol cloud the way I see myself anymore. Alcohol happened to me but it doesn't define me. I am so much more than that. And I am determined to be less critical of 25 year old Gina. Because like all the other Ginas, that one did her best. She had a kind heart and she was in pain; she blew with the wind. I want 26 year old Gina to be strong like an oak tree. To take all the things that have happened and use them to put down roots. To turn them into strength. And to love herself, even with all the imperfections.

5/24/16 I've heard it said that life is like a hike and I couldn't agree more. Sometimes you're in a valley and sometimes you're on a summit. Sometimes you're in a clearing and you can see way into the distance. Other times, you're in a dense forest and you can hardly see one step ahead. Sometimes the trail takes on a steep incline and it's a lot more strenuous to keep moving forward. And sometimes when the trail is headed downhill it is effortless and easy to know where you place your foot next. We all hike through muck to get to where we are going. Social media creates this illusion that everyone else lives on peaks. So we feel bummed when we compare other people's peaks with our messy trail. But everyone else isn't a peak all the time. They just don't share the messy times. If you're trudging through muck right now, you're not alone. It will get better, circumstances are fleeting. No two paths are alike, so try not to compare your journey to anyone else's. Because it is going to be different. And that's perfectly okay. Take comfort in the fact that you are exactly where you should be. You are headed in the right direction. The only trick is to just keep putting one foot in front of the other. And remind yourself that your story is not over; it doesn't end in the mud or on the steep incline. Every step, every minute, every breath is bringing you closer to your clearing and closer to your summit.

Twenty-five year old Gina reminds me that life doesn't end in the muck. She gives me courage to keep trudging. She reminds me that no matter how alone I feel in my situation, I am never alone. She was never alone. Her secret made her feel isolated but statistics tell a different story. As did the support group. The other women were like her. They are everywhere. But she didn't know. She thought she was alone on Broken Island.

My favorite thing about her was watching God restore her. He didn't scrap her and leave her in hell, then construct a polished version of her. He brought her out with all of her cracks, and He poured love into those cracks and He mended her from the inside out. The seams from the cracks are a reminder of God's unfailing, unconditional love. The seams are a reminder that she is resilient, therefore, I am resilient. Even on days when I don't feel it one bit, on days when that distant memory seems too far away, and on days when it feels like God is quiet. The restored and updated version of Gina is no better nor more worthy than the younger edition. God improved her and built upon her. She is just as worthy as I am today. And others. She did her best the way I do my best today. She made choices to the best of her ability. She was in constant agonizing pain. How could I fault her for seeking comfort?

> 2/1/15 I like to think of the time I spent drowning in the bottom of a bottle as the machine that washed the judgmental asshole out of me. Unfortunately, I got stuck on the spin cycle for a few extra years.

Jesus didn't wait until I was presentable and cleaned up to love me and come scoop me up to save me. He didn't leave Drunk Gina to rot and make a new one. He came into my muddy hellish prison of a pit and loved me through it. He held my hand as He escorted me out. He was with me the entire time. He never once passed judgment; only love. Sweet, sweet love.

I not only forgave Drunk Gina, but I came to love and treasure her. It has been a process to embrace and accept that chapter of my life. Part of me wants to sweep it under the rug and then part of me wants to put it in a display case. I do not regret it. I would never want to experience it again but if God showed up and asked me if I wanted to redo my life and skip it, I would have to tell Him, "No thanks." I used to think that life was black and white. I used to be judgmental and critical of people. Through failing myself, I got to the point where I realized that my best efforts were not enough. I began to extend this same gentle compassion on to others.

> 2/3/15 Back when I was only 18 in June of 2007 I wrote this entry about how I felt discontent and drinking only increased that I wrote then that alcohol kills my growth. And that it cuts my roots and makes me drift miserably. And that it's all just a grand distraction that buries discontentment
>
> How different my life may have been had I fucking drank the coffee then.

But I also made a list of the type of person I want to be. (Kind, self-assured, able to identify with others, none-judgmental, relatable, conversational, funny, peaceful, etc.) And through life, I've gained many of those characteristics. And it was in the places where I bumped my head that shaped me into be the type of person I wanted to be. So I should focus on the positive outcomes from not drinking the coffee sooner.

Sometimes, I look back at that chapter and I realize I'm a different person today. But I can glance in the mirror, and I can feel that girl's heart beating inside of my chest. I remember how it stung every day. I remember how badly she wanted to simply be held. When I think of her today, I love on her. I hug her, I envelop her in grace and love. I tell her that she was enough and that if it wasn't for her perseverance, I wouldn't be the strong fighter I am today. That girl walked through hell. She spent years in the fire. And she made it out the other side. She wasn't pathetic or weak. She was a warrior! I couldn't do it today. I don't think I would be strong enough. But she was. I am grateful to her for that. I want her to be here today to witness where life will take me. I want her to know that her struggle wasn't for nothing. I want her to know I value and treasure her, flaws and all. I want her to see that the areas of her greatest weaknesses are cloaked under my greatest strengths. When I step out in fear, I do it for her and for all the Lukes out there today. When I tell my story, I do it for them. I think of them, and I muster up courage. Because that's what they deserve.

Drunk Gina did her absolute best and it was enough! It was more than enough. Her memory is my Golden Globe, my medal, my trophy. Her memory is also my hope. When things get tough, and they do get tough, she reminds me that they can get better. She reminds me that no matter how tough life gets, always try again. Always push through one more day.

Gina Mast
October 28, 2015 · 🌐

There seems to be a misconception about love: that each one of us has a limited supply of love in our hearts. We hold onto it with a death grip, not wanting to waste it on the wrong people or the wrong things. The truth is that love is similar to time in that they are both perishable goods. What you don't use is lost. The only wasted love is the unexpressed kind. The thing about love is that the more you give it away, the more your supply multiplies. You don't need to hoard your love. It's okay to give plentifully and to give freely. You'll only get more.

> *I began to post words of truth in an attempt to encourage others like me who were still fighting the battle. I wanted to share strength and hope with everyone who needed it.*

CHAPTER 12

So This is Trust?

I SAW A GUY ON the first day at the coed meeting who caught my eye. But I knew a relationship was the last thing I needed. I was still detoxing at this point. I don't know how long it takes, but after years of abuse, I felt like I was still full of chemicals even though it had been eight days. I stayed clear of any men during this time. I focused on female relationships. These women welcomed me with open arms. Everyone was loving, supportive and friendly. They made me feel like I was lovable and gave me a place to belong to. They gave me sober things to do and sober people to do the things with.

I worked through a twelve-step program and continued to find peace in life. I was unpacking the baggage I'd been carrying and I was sorting out the suitcases. I was throwing away the items I no longer needed, I was folding the items I wanted to keep, and I was organizing it all. I was in a really good place.

Fast forward a few months and I had a dream about the cute guy who I noticed on day one. Essentially, we went skydiving together. So I knew that I would be taking some type of leap with him because I believed that skydiving was a metaphor for taking a plunge. I wasn't sure exactly what this meant. The thought crossed my mind that perhaps the hottie had been a placeholder for this guy. Since he was married and I was here alone. Maybe I was allowed to have those dreams so that I would wait for this guy right here? Maybe the plunge meant falling in love? I didn't know but I was open to taking the leap of faith. I didn't know what the outcome would be, but I knew God was with me.

About a month after the dream, he asked me out on a date. Going on my first sober date was almost as exhilarating as skydiving. I had no buffers.

It was completely raw. I was nervous and jittery. I had nothing to numb it or help me calm down. But you know what? It was amazing. The date itself wasn't because I couldn't even swallow my salad since my stomach thought it would be a good idea to fold itself inside out and hang out in my throat. But I felt alive, I felt what it means to live! I felt everything. I felt the anxiety. I felt shy but I worked through the shyness.

Learning to live without alcohol was hard. Not just the habit. The toughest nights where I missed it the most were lonely Sunday nights. And times when I was doing housework like laundry or cleaning. Because that's boring shit. I missed it as a crutch during social situations. I had to feel the fear, face it, and work through it without anything other than courage.

I have learned to develop true courage, which is one of my favorite things. Alcohol gave me a false sense of courage. Living without it required that I learn to develop or tap into real, raw courage. Clammy hands, trembling limbs, red cheeked showing up. I try to remind myself that God is with me. Sometimes I feel it. Sometimes I don't. But I show up anyways. Courage isn't always feeling brave and strong; it's feeling scared and nervous but going anyways.

2/25/15 I had a dream last night. There was a little bird. For some reason, it didn't know it could fly. The bird was crossing a huge canyon. There was a ladder that jutted out over a tiny portion of the canyon. And there was a ladder on the far side of the canyon. But there was a HUGE gap between the ladders. The bird walked to the end of the ladder and somehow it supernaturally crossed the canyon and made it to the other side. If a bird knew it could fly, it wouldn't have used the ladders to try to bridge the gap. It would have flown from land to land. But the bird still made it to the other side even though it didn't know it could fly. I felt like God filled in the gaps for me. I did things the best I could, and when I couldn't do any more, He raised the ground to meet my feet as I walked. If someone asked me how I got sober, I would have to say this is a great way to summarize it. I did the best I could, then God did the rest. Because there are areas that I'm unable to explain. It's like one day I was on one side of the canyon. I did the best that I knew. Then another day, I wound up on the other side of the canyon. And I credit God for bridging the gap for me and transporting me over to the far side.]

I was the best version of myself during this relationship. I was able to work through all the fear I'd always had. I let him into my closet where he could see the things from my past. It wasn't easy, it was hard. But I was able to. We did it in steps. He made me feel safe, I let him in. Further and further. He got me. Our relationship was easy, direct, and fun. This was the most selfless and unconditionally loving that I've been yet. It was the most mature relationship I've had the privilege to be a part of. I was able to learn about his past and leave it in the past, without holding it against him. Because I too have a past. And I know that if someone were to look at it, they wouldn't have an accurate picture of the person that I am today.

Throughout the relationship, I was experiencing anxiety. I thought it was just fear so I tried to push through it. I had several dreams about him indicating that he may not have had pure motives, that he wasn't one to accept responsibility for his actions, and that he was going to bail on me. These dreams didn't align with what I was seeing at all. So I noted them but I filed them away in my journals. I didn't make any decisions based off of these dreams.

The one day, I was driving in the car and I asked God if he was "the one" for me. Within minutes, my phone rang:

7/27/15 Dad called over lunch to tell me not to settle. "Don't hold on to something because you're afraid there won't be something better. Wait until you know it's the right one who was made for you."

This answered my question. When I asked myself if my fears were actually doubts that he was right for me, my heart said yes. But my mind panicked. I didn't want to be the last person standing alone. I didn't want to be the only single one. I wanted to have kids and a family and a future. So I questioned my peace. I convinced myself that maybe it was just fear even though my gut knew the truth. I didn't want to agree with it so I fought my gut. I didn't want to go back to being alone. I was now nearing 27 and I wanted to get married so I could have my first kid by the time I was 30. I tried to let go of my original timeline. Without realizing it, I was creating another timeline. I still thought I had lost time to make up for. The idea of being single made me squirm because I didn't want to wait any longer. I was sober. I was emotionally in a good place and according to my opinion, it was time! It was time. It was time.

When it came to discussing the future, he had walls up. There were things from his past that hindered and affected his future decisions. I had been praying about it with no direction or clarity. When we arrived at a point in our relationship, I laid things out for him. I told him that I needed him to step back and kind of figure things out on his end. Because there was no moving forward until he removed the roadblocks in his own path. I was terrified of the outcome.

3/15/15 Dad called. He woke me up to tell me God is saving me. He's holding me for someone specific. So I don't run around with chickens when I can fly with eagles.

A phone call several days later notified me that he didn't feel able to give me the future I wanted. Having kids was something I dreamed about. And due to his divorce, he wasn't open to having any more children. I wanted to change his mind and convince him of hope in a bright future! But I couldn't. Before that phone call, I had been sitting on the floor talking to God, because this is what I do with my Papa God. We have informal chats all the time where I share my heart with Him and let Him share His heart with me. During this particular chat, I had told Him "This is in Your hands. Whichever way it goes, I'm giving it to You. If it works out, I'll know he is right for me. If it doesn't, I'll let it go."

While I was sad, it gave me peace to leave my hands off of the situation. I went to a new church the evening after the breakup and the pastor said something like, "There is someone here whose relationship failed. God wants you to know you did everything you could. He wants you to give it to Him and let it go." God was letting me know He had me and He knew where I was. It still hurt but there was peace in the pain. God was in the middle of it; tagging along with me. When I couldn't sleep and walked at night, He walked with me. When I fell into pieces, He helped me collect myself. My heart ached but He filled up the seams once again with love.

The main incentive I had for sobering up was my future; I wanted love and a relationship in my life. Here I was, a week shy from my one year Soberversary and I had lost the thing I wanted the most. It had fallen through my fingers. Despite this, the desire to drink didn't antagonize me or even cross my mind. I knew that whatever I was feeling would only be worsened by alcohol. I knew that it would delay the pain and only increase it exponentially. I let myself have ice cream. I knew I was using food to cope with pain but I felt safe doing this in the short term. Jesus held me through the long nights, the sleeplessness and the waves of pain.

God brought me fresh hope regularly. I had another dream about the hottie. It left me feeling hopeful that one day I'll meet someone like him, who affects me the way he does. Several days after the breakup, my sister from Florida called. She had a dream that she came to meet Kamal. But when she came out to meet him, it wasn't him. It was someone else. She saw me happy and bubbly. Only then did I tell her about the breakup, which no one saw coming. Because I have a tendency to be doubtful, God found yet another way to show me that He knew it had happened and that He had someone else for me that would come into my life with time. I discovered that the pain would come. I discovered that it would take my breath away and hurt my ribs. I also discovered that if I didn't run from it, if I sat there and let it hurt, it went away again. Thinking about the pain was worse than experiencing the pain. When I stopped fearing it, it lost some of its power.

This was my first sober wedding. The one bartender kept coming over to me and trying to get me to drink in a poor attempt to flirt with me. I was probably the only sober person at the wedding and I was one of the few people not dancing.

I felt uptight because I didn't have a buffer for the anxiety I felt. The friend who I was there with didn't know about my drinking issue; she only knew that I wasn't drinking that weekend. I finally went in the bathroom and called my sister and talked to her for a while to calm down. When we were leaving, I went back in and came clean with the bartender. I asked him to consider that someone is trying to practice sobriety so that he lays off the pressure. I was fine. But the next person might not have been. He probably just didn't know. Or maybe he thought I didn't look like someone who had the need to practice sobriety.

CHAPTER 13

Where You Go, I'll Go

My decision to pursue a relationship had strained the relationship I had with my mentor. She had been applying pressure for me to do things a particular way. I wasn't doing things her way and I could tell this was frustrating her. She always questioned my motives. When I sent anonymous concert tickets to Bayn in the mail, she was convinced I was trying to reconcile with him. The truth? I found out his dad died. I sent him two tickets because I knew he wouldn't spend the money on them. I figured he could invite a girl and feel special. I was hoping he would feel God's love through the tickets. I can love someone without being in love with someone; I can love someone without wanting them back. But she wasn't able to see that others approached life differently than her.

During the breakup, I had consulted God. She was upset that she found out about the breakup after the fact. To her, my going to God wasn't satisfactory. She wanted to be the in-between. I understand her concern about my decisions that were made independently, but Jesus is a very present part of my life. And if I have a direct line to God, why would I call an operator when I can call His direct extension? She and I had two different relationships with our maker, which is why she questioned the security of mine. I believe she did the right thing, she just did not understand.

She laid off the pressure for about a month during the breakup but then it started again. It was unbearable. "Get down on your knees and pray every day." (But my God is chill, He sits beside me. I love Him because He loves me. It's not a formal BS façade. He doesn't require me to put space between us. He holds my hand. When I cry, He holds me like the five-year-old child that

I feel like.) "Call me every day. Work on the steps more. You're not working enough. You need to go to more meetings. You need to talk to more people. Ask women out for coffee. Make more sober friends."

> 9/10/15 When you're feeling impatient, remember: you can't rush a flower to bloom. You can try to add extra sunlight or you can try to add extra water or you can try to force the pedals open... But doing any of these things won't actually help, it'll simply harm the damn flower. Some things require time.

The place that had once been my refuge had become a different breed of monkey on my back. It had become the agony in my life. I had spent so many nights crying, feeling like I was going to spontaneously combust from all the pressure. I kept asking God to fix the relationship with my mentor and to remove this pressure. But He didn't. Because He had other plans. I just didn't know about them at the time.

Nobody in the group mentioned the J word, or Jesus. They thought we should keep our spiritual views general so that they mesh with anyone's beliefs, which I get the point of. But Jesus is my story. I can't tell my story and leave Him out. I think that God comes to us in many forms; He speaks our language. He comes however we receive Him. I was familiar with the story of Jesus. I don't know if He would've sent another representative if I didn't believe in Jesus. But Jesus did come; He is real to me.

The more involved I became in the support group, the more I felt as though my views were clashing with theirs. Starting each meeting by proclaiming my false identity felt wrong. When I say false identity, I'm referring to the way I had been identifying with my habits and circumstances, rather than identifying as the person who God made me to be. I'm talking about claiming *it* and *it's* set of lies as my identity. God said I have a spirit of power, therefore, I am not powerless or weak. He made me whole, therefore, I am not broken or sick. God gave me the power to speak life and death; this helped me slay the dragon in the first place. Why was I affirming this lie each time I complied with this custom? Instead of proclaiming healing and truth, I was being told to latch back onto the lie and claiming to still be sick by saying I am still a slave to it. Essentially, I was feeding the beast which had attempted to kill me. I was playing nice with it; trying to recognize its power because of fear that *it* would come back to swipe me away into the abyss. Instead of stating that through God, I have been healed, I was declaring that I was in fact still sick.

I felt like I couldn't truly be myself, yet I was fearful of leaving. After asking God about it for months, I had a dream. I was on an airplane with the group. And we were taxiing down the highway. Airplanes can taxi but they are meant to fly! They go much faster in the air, not crawling on the ground. What I got from it was that there is an easier way to do things. That way works but it is slow. It made me feel like a bird in a cage.

I grew up in religion and even well-meaning secular groups with rules can be religious. Fear can keep anyone in a safety net. But sometimes there isn't a big difference between a safety net and a cage. The assignments from the group made me feel like I was paying penance to live. Like, now that I was okay, I had to keep working every day to stay okay or the beast would come back and destroy me. But the beast was dead, the dragon was slayed, the blood was shed. The fight was over, the war was won. Jesus got me sober so I trust Him to keep me sober.

So if the Son sets you free, you will be free indeed. John 8:36 NIV

Almost a year to the day after I wrote in my journal, "God, I'll go to the support group unless You lead me otherwise" it was time for me to move on. Still, after hearing every day, "If you leave, you'll get drunk" I was scared to go. I knew God was with me, but I still needed something more concrete. I told Him "God, I'm scared. You're going to have to take it out of my hands." Within a short time, my mentor called me. She told me that she wasn't going to be able to help me anymore; letting me know I would need to find another mentor who could work with me. This was my golden ticket. This was my answered prayer. I was still scared but I knew God had me. That night I went to a worship service I rarely attended. I would go when I was scared or in pain.

My heart was asking, "Do you really have me, God? Are You sure You have me?" They played a song called *Shepherd*:

> "You will lift my head above the mighty waves, You are able to keep me from stumbling. And in my weakness, You are the strength that comes from within. Good shepherd of my soul, take my hand and lead me on.
>
> You make my footsteps and my path secure, so walking on water is just the beginning. Cause my faith to arise, stand at attention for You are calling me to greater things."

The lyrics spoke to my heart and brought tears to my eyes. This was God's way of saying, "I see you Gina. I have you. I will lead you and protect you and keep you." It was once again time for me to move on.

I had returned to racing as I built up my health and fitness. I ran a half marathon in July with a little over nine months of sobriety under my belt. I wanted to set a new personal record so that I could have evidence that my body have recovered. I wanted to know I hadn't done irreparable damage. I didn't even match my existing PR, coming in at 1:58:45. About a month after the breakup, I ran another half in Savannah, at about thirteen months sober. Despite the 100% humidity, the 70 degrees temperature by 5 a.m. and the race officials calling the race due to a heat advisory, I set a new PR. By nearly ten minutes. 1:51:15. I had asked God to bless my run just for the sake of blessing it and He did. He was my strength. He was with me, in every step. He always shows up. I had been better trained for the Chicago half. I had put in all my efforts and it wasn't enough to set a PR. I showed up at the Savannah half underprepared and I knew it. And He showed up, like He always does. I guess that's what it means when they say His strength is made perfect in our weakness. I get it now.

Hopelust

Doing what it says I'm doing: running a race.

CHAPTER 14

A Sense of Identity

THE BEST WAY TO SUMMARIZE what I learned from *it* is to look at the dream I had about giants on 7/3/13. In it, Jesus never left my side. Heaven sent angels to protect me and fight off giants I didn't even know existed. The giant that got close to me was alcohol. Jesus stayed with me the entire time and coached me on how to defeat it. Defeating the giant did not require skill or wit; the only requirement was standing my ground. Simply standing in my true identity enabled my arms to push through the center of the giant and it tumbled down.

Jesus could've easily destroyed this giant before it reached me. But instead, He taught me who I am in Him. He taught me how to overcome this giant because He wanted me to realize my power. He wanted to show me that I am empowered, capable, brave, and strong. Talk about beauty for ashes! I get to live a life that is carefree and I don't have to fear giants or bad circumstances. I now know how to defeat a giant. I am able to live from victory, knowing that simply standing on His words and His promises will change the circumstances and change the facts. I know from first-hand experience that my words truly do have the power to speak life and death. I know that He sees me as perfect, pure, righteous, whole, innocent, and free. He doesn't look at my false identities shaped by my actions, He looks at my heart and He sees me as flawless. He is love. He loves the bad out of me and He loves the pain away. He fills my heart with light, which leaves no room for darkness. If a lion misidentifies itself as a kitten, it can spend its life in fear, being antagonized by endless predators. But when a lion learns it is a lion, life is never the same again. A lion walks around like the king that it is, full of courage. Knowing that God is with me gives me this courage.

Jesus was with me every day but *it* finally made me aware of His presence in my life. He transformed my heaviest burden into my most treasured blessing. The biggest lie led me to the most significant truth. My darkest hour led me into my brightest morning. I am aware of glory in places I never knew existed. The process has allowed me to remove the weight of fear. When I see Him, I don't fear. When my perspective is off, He corrects it so that I can again remove this backpack of fear.

Life has continued to happen. I continue to grow. Growth is about continuously taking plunges and trying new experiences. I don't think I'll ever arrive at an age where I'm done growing. There is a lesson to be learned from water: running rivers stay clean. It's the water sitting still in swamps that fosters bacteria. I try to find balance where I have enough time to reflect but also have enough adventures that keep stretching me.

Sometimes growth is as simple as challenging myself to try a new restaurant solo, other times it is sitting down and having a difficult conversation. I seek growth because fresh growth brings fresh water and fresh life. Growth breaks the dams in life and allows new water to gush down into the slowing stream.

Today, if you asked me who I am, I would be able to provide an answer because I know who I am. I am a pursuer of peace, a seeker of truth, an appreciator of truth and a lover of kindness. I'm not certain what words I would use to describe myself in a year from now because I'm constantly discovering and evolving.

Every day isn't perfect. But even on the not-so-good days, I have gratitude, which leads to joy and peace. I am grateful that I can drive to work without feeling like Charlize Theron in her Monster role. I am grateful that my head doesn't hurt and that I'm not experiencing the shakes every day. I'm grateful that I don't have to hide anymore. I'm grateful that I can make eye contact with a stranger without worrying that they will see into my soul. I'm grateful that I can live in the light. I'm grateful that when I have a bad day, I can openly and honestly tell someone what is paining me. I'm grateful that I'm no longer isolated. I'm grateful that I experience peace on most days. I'm grateful that my body is repairing itself every day instead of continuing to wreck itself. I'm grateful that I'm headed toward a better tomorrow. I'm grateful for the opportunities life offers. I'm grateful for hope. And I'm grateful that through my horrific experience with *it*, I developed a relationship with my Heavenly Father. I came home to Papa God.

I have not arrived at my final destination, life has only just begun. There will be challenges that I will work through in the future, but I know with certainty that God is for me. And if He is for me, no challenge can overcome me. He is my riser. In Him, if I get something wrong, I will stand up and try again. And again. And again. And again. Because He designed me to persevere.

He's my strength. He's my constant, He's my happiness, He's my peace and He's my joy. He's my wisdom, He's my guidance and He is everything to me. He is my hope. He is my tomorrows. He is my faith. When I struggle to see through the lie that I am alone, I let God simply hold me in His strong arms the way a perfect father would; especially when I am too weak to stand. When my heart hurts, He brings me comfort. When I can't even put my fears into words, He soothes my pain. When I don't understand and I feel a fire in my chest from frustration, He holds me and lets me throw my temper tantrum. I used to think, "OMG, Gina! You can't talk to God like that. You can't tell Him you're angry or yell at Him." One time, after a blowup, I was beating myself up for losing my shit once again. And He let me know that my temper was one of His favorite things about me; He likes my thunder. He doesn't like cleaned up, canned, fake crap. He likes real, raw, honest conversation. He doesn't get mad when I express my anger. Instead, He blankets my fears with love. Then He does this again the next day and the next. Because I'm a human and I forget. He waits for me to calm down and shows up again with love and helps correct my perspective to help me see that He is bigger than any circumstance, challenge, or feeling.

As I go through my day, I ask Him to show me He sees me and remind me that I am where I should be. Sometimes I see blatant affection on billboards and writing on trucks, sometimes I hear a song on the radio with lyrics that are from Him – an answer to the prayer I just prayed. Sometimes it's a sign through people, even a stranger. Sometimes, I hear a whisper in my heart that I just know is Him. He reaches me in a million different ways. Sometimes I ask Him to give me a treasure hunt. I go through my day searching and collecting signs of His love for me.

> 8/1/16 Sometimes you have to let the circumstances be what they are and go play. Do something that thrills you and makes your heart pound. The things that are beyond your control will sort themselves out but you don't need to sit and watch the paint dry.

There are some things I have yet to understand, like the situation with the hottie. There are nights when I struggle with confusion. I meet someone and I compare him to this character who has been a companion in my dreams and who has become a part of my life over the last few years. Even today, it's the fall of 2016 and I continue having dreams about the hottie from time to time. I see him around and I hide. Because I feel like I know him so well and he's practically a stranger. Sometimes I ask God, "Why? Was it to give me hope? Was it so that I wait for the right guy? Was he a space holder for someone else?"

> 8/22/16 The most precious kind of peace is the kind found through complete trust prior to the desired outcome/conclusion of the story.

I honestly don't know why. But it's okay; I don't need to hold onto this question with a death grip. Sometimes chasing the "Why?" is a lot like a dog chasing its tail in the sense that it doesn't get you anywhere. Fear and trust cannot coexist; where there is trust, there is no room for fear. Though I do not entirely understand, I trust that He will work it out for my good. Because that's what He does. He's done it in the past and He will do it in my future. He's my Rescuer, my Redeemer, my Protector, and my Keeper. He is my loving Father, who cares for me in every single area of my life. With Him, there is no lack, only fullness. In the area of my heart where loneliness once resided, He resides and He pumps so much love into my heart that it overflows onto those around me. There is an overabundance of love. He lavishes me with affection. The one thing I desired from humanity and craved all my life was found in Him.

What was once the need for a relationship has become a simple desire. I'm no longer looking for a man to come save me, I've been saved. I no longer need someone to take me under his wing because I have my own wings. I am interested in finding a counterpart. I'm interested in taking the world on headfirst and forging ahead into the future. I'm interested in making waves and in extending a hand back into the pit that I came through, to make a chain-link of arms to help out others in that place.

 **Gina Mast**
January 24

Several years ago, a strong, brave, courageous woman unknowingly helped me see hope during a very dark period in my life. She did this by making herself vulnerable and sharing the loss of her brother publicly. We had worked together one summer when I was 18 and we didn't interact since. Yet her posts shed light into my darkness. And for that reason, I have courage to share these posts, hoping it will help someone who is currently stuck in their darkness. Thank you,  You continue to inspire me.

> **Hopelust**
> January 24
>
> When you look at her from the outside,
> It seems like she's had it easy,
> Her exterior looks co... Continue Reading

Sharing some of my favorite things: hope and authenticity.

CHAPTER 15

Living a Life of Love

I KNOW THAT THE MORE flexible we become, the more unbreakable we become. Life can be messy and confusing and complicated. I now know to allow room for the detours, even when I don't understand why they occur. And I know to allow room for the mess, the confusion, and the complicated parts. When I remain flexible, I'm able to adjust accordingly without getting plowed over by circumstances. I strive to be like a little sailboat that goes with the wind and actually uses it to gain momentum instead of throwing down my anchor and getting pummeled by the waves. I know that one day I will understand; one day I will see how the challenge at hand led me to an even greater victory. Because that's what challenges do: they raise us to higher levels. They upgrade our lives. Every challenge or problem is restored exponentially, which means that each challenge will lead to a better tomorrow.

I try to tell myself what I wish Gina-In-The-Washer would've known. While some circumstances take time to change, my peace and joy are not contingent on that outcome. Pat Summitt once said, "It is what it is, but it will be what you make it." I get to choose what I want to do with each day. I can dwell on the things in life that I want to change and I can make a list of the things I don't have yet. Or I can choose to cultivate gratitude. I can choose to find ways to bless others, so that I in turn am blessed. I think this is commonly referred to as selfish giving. But everyone wins so I think it is okay.

Last fall, I was getting some coffee at Starbucks in the Target at North Hills. There was a well-dressed lady in line in front of me. I felt that inner nudge to buy her coffee. My rational brain noticed her appearance and noted that she didn't look like she needed the money for a $2.00 coffee. But the nudge persisted, so I did it. She was shocked and taken aback. I felt awkward because I interrupted her checkout to add her order to my tab. She stared at me as I paid. Then she asked me what my name was; her name was Sarah. I told her my mom's name was Sarah. At that point, tears poured from her eyes. She had lost a daughter to brain cancer a short time ago and she always missed her daughter during the holidays. God didn't nudge me to buy her coffee because she needed the money, He wanted her to know that He sees her and He wanted to hug her heart. When she cried, I cried. We stood there, two complete strangers, hugging each other and crying together.

After that incident, I'm much quicker to follow that nudging. One time at Whole Foods, I was at the checkout and I felt the nudging to buy a bouquet of flowers and give them to the grouchy cashier. My brain told me, "She's being so rude! Why would I do that?" I heard "Do it anyway." Again, "What if she thinks I'm weird? I don't know her." I heard "Do it anyway." I paid for my dinner and the flowers. The girl's eyes got big. She seemed confused and then she told me that nobody had ever bought her flowers before. They say that we need love the most when we deserve it the least, and this situation was why. She was acting mean. But God saw her heart and knew that love would bring out her best. I glanced in the store front as I drove away to see her crying into another cashier's shoulder. I don't know what her situation was but I don't need to know. I only know God wanted her to know He loved her.

I read an entry in the "Loved by God" devotional that Women of Faith produced. It said something about a Bible verse suggesting you shouldn't let your right hand see what your left hand is doing. In other words, you should give without letting others see. It said that secrets have power. So keep the good things a secret and let the bad things out into the light. I try to put my energy into showing love so that I can lighten the load someone else is carrying. So now, when I'm having a rough day and I struggle to have the correct perspective, I ask God who He wants to bless. Then I do random things for random people. Obviously, I can't write about the things I continue to do. But

I can say that it is fun to watch the random assortment of unconnected people that God chooses to love on. This can put meaning into every single day.

I used to think my life would not have meaning or significance until I met my significance other and started a family. I used to think I wouldn't mean anything or have a purpose until then, but that has completely changed. Sure, there are days when I forget that I am not alone. But this is a temporary season in my life. God has given me dreams of my wedding day and He has found a million ways to show me that I'll be happy in the future with a relationship. But how much would my story mean if I was able to get sober only after I got what I wanted? Maybe God wanted me to see that He could make it happen without the thing I wanted. That He was able to show me that on my own, I am strong, courageous, brave, independent and whole. He showed me that I don't need anyone else to complete me because He completes me. He showed me that I am able to push through fear on my own, I don't need another hand to hold mine. I can survive the dark night. I am able to withstand discomfort.

Embracing singleness has been a process, like all things. I know that God has me and I know He is working out the future for my good. What can I do about being single? Every time I have heard from God regarding a timeline for my future husband, I heard "Wait for a complete and perfect time." I know that some things are within my authority to speak over, but I don't think this is one of those things because every time I have asked Him about it, He has said "Wait."

So what can I do? I can hate being single and I can live my life in my room awaiting the day that it is time. Or I can change the questions I ask God, I can change my approach at handling singleness. I want to learn to love and treasure it. I want to learn to see the good in it.

When it's snowing in the winter, it wouldn't be appropriate to fight the cold temperature. It would be stupid to go outside without the proper clothing and curse the cold. It is more sensible to adjust our wardrobe selection. It would be more appropriate to bundle up until the winter passes. This makes it a lot more comfortable while we await warmer temperatures. What if we did this with challenging situations in life? What if we didn't fight them but adjusted so that we could learn from them? What if we made our challenge a friend instead of loathing it? We do the best we can with the things that are within our control, then make peace with the things that are outside of our authority. His wisdom lets us know what is within our control and what isn't. This changes with every situation.

Why do I want a relationship right now? I want a partner. I want strength and shelter. I want peace and companionship. I can ask God to be those things. He has been those things, but I can ask Him to continue giving me the awareness that He is those things. What if God doesn't want me to be hidden in a relationship? What if He wants to make me strong on my own? If I had met someone prior to writing this book, I might not have written it. I might have been content with life where I was and not been willing to risk my reputation if it could potentially be reflected on someone close to me. Being in my shoes, I don't have to check with my spouse to see if it's cool that I open up about my mess to the world.

I've been asking God what He wants to be for me in this time of singleness. And the answer is that He wants to be my everything. He wants to be my comforter, my savior, my strength, my shelter. He wants to make me whole. He wants to be all the things for me that I want from a relationship. He wants to make me strong on my own so that other individuals can see that they too are complete on their own.

I think God wanted to wait until I saw that He is my other half; that He completes me. He didn't want me to need anyone other than Him. It's nice to have people and want them, but needing someone adds a pressure nobody wants to live with. God wanted me to see that He supplies every single thing I want. He wanted me to see that I am never alone.

I look forward to being married. I look forward to having a family and some kiddos. I look forward to having someone to pick me up at the airport after a trip. I look forward to having someone to miss while I'm away. I look forward to having someone to come home to and try to cook with. I look forward to having someone who can remind me that I'm a lion on days when I feel like a kitten. But my life isn't on hold until that day. My life is now. My life is today. There are chapters in my life that are yet to be written prior to the one where I join up with my soul mate. I'll be doing my thing, finding my own way in the world in the meantime.

I can spend my free time and allow God to use me like a riverbed that lets love flow through me. God is the one who creates love, I'm merely the vessel that allows it to flow through me. That's why I never run out of love. He's the supplier. If I didn't know that, I would build a dam to hoard and contain love. Instead of giving it away freely to anyone around.

I'm a human and I'm no saint. I get mad at people. I impulsively wave my middle finger at bad drivers, then five minutes later I beat myself up for losing my cool. I'm sure Mother Teresa never flipped off a driver. Then again, she probably never drove herself around. So it's okay. The point isn't to be perfect. The point is that there is mercy for every one of my shortcomings. I don't make messes intentionally. But when I do, I know Who will help me clean them up.

From what I've seen about my future husband, he will know God the same way I do. And that's the only way a relationship could work for me. I need someone who can fly alone. Instead of demanding that God brings my significant other right now, I want to know what He wants to do with me in the meantime. What does He want to do with me today that He couldn't do if I was married? He has my full attention, all my time, and all my energy.

I always associated the word single with the word waiting. And the idea of waiting made me panic and squirm. I craved patience but I didn't want to develop it. I never asked God to make my life meaningful now. I never asked Him to make the most of this time being single. I never asked Him to help me find the joy in being single.

When I heard the word wait, I used to hear "Sit still, hold." Waiting is none of these things. Waiting is living. Waiting is moving and growing and being. Waiting is journeying and exploring. Waiting is learning and thriving independently. Waiting means waiting to give someone the title of husband or wife, it doesn't mean waiting to live. It means waiting until we meet the person we know God handpicked for us. In the meantime, I can grow to be independent. I can be a champion of singleness. I can speak truth into loneliness.

Waiting on timing is like managing a wild horse. If you fight it, it'll drag you around through the dirt. It'll hurt and be painful. And there is nothing you can do to control it. If you accept and embrace it, you can ride the horse. The view will be better, the ride will be more enjoyable. And you'll learn to use it as momentum to move you where you should be.

7/22/16 In the place where you want to crawl out of your own skin, that's where the growth happens.

If God got me sober through the worst season of my life, then surely He is able to keep me during any future winters. He's magical like that. When I forget miracles do happen, and I do because I'm human and I get consumed with the distractions of the day, I look at my sobriety counter. I have an app on my phone. When I see how many days it's been since I stopped drinking, I remember miracles are real. And when I start worrying about my future, I remember that, "Surely, if He had me then, He has me now."

Back when I couldn't picture a life without alcohol, I would have wanted to ask someone practicing sobriety if they missed drinking. Or if they ever arrived in a place where they didn't miss alcohol anymore. Sometimes I miss the idea of drinking in moderation. But I don't miss drinking the way it actually was. I miss the idea of having a drink on a date or getting a buzz at a concert. But I don't miss actual memories of this. Because my memories don't include these things. I don't miss blacking out on a third date and crying about something bad that happened to me. I don't miss passing out at concerts or dancing with strangers at concerts and not knowing who saw me. I don't miss waking up to expensive receipts in my wallet from drinks at bars, pizza orders and cab rides. I don't miss the crippling fear of not knowing what I'd done. My drinking was never normal or moderate. I don't miss my drinking.

Gina Mast added 2 new photos — at ♀ **Chimney Tops**.
June 19

At the top of the scariest summit I have ever reached. The summit profile pic is from Google. I was too distracted to take pics during the ascent.

Not pictured: self-doubt, fear, sucked back tears, trembling, heart pounding,... See More

Sharing the inside and the outside of the truth in a post. I try to post honest things that let people know they aren't alone. I try to include the whole truth.

CHAPTER 16

Journal Entry 9/30/2016

I've been sober for two years today. I am free. I live my life out in the open. Open enough to share my story in the hopes that it'll help someone else. I don't spend my time doing damage control of situations that transpired during blackouts. I haven't had to order a duplicate ID or hunt down missing credit cards and keys. I don't have to compartmentalize my life for fear that others will find out about my shenanigans. I don't hide mystery bruises because of fear that I'll be asked about their origin and it'll be apparent that I am clueless in that regard. I'm not afraid to make medical appointments anymore because there isn't a deep dark secret to discover in reviewing my health. I don't have to eat minced garlic for breakfast to cover my breath. I'm okay with people sitting close to me. I don't have to drink coffee and pretend that I am jittery to distract from the fact that I have the shakes. I don't have to hide my flushed cheeks and nose under makeup. I rarely have a headache, a stomach ache or get sick otherwise.

I can, at the drop of a hat, pick up and drive anywhere. I'm no longer confined to my apartment nor am I confined to that god forsaken bottle. I don't have to create plans to enable drinking in every situation. I no longer make calculations about how to keep the withdrawal symptoms at bay. I don't miss out on happenings because of being passed out. If I choose not to participate in an event, it's by choice and not because I slept through it involuntarily. I can schedule an appointment weeks or months in advance and know that I'll be able to keep it. I won't be too disoriented from withdrawal nor will I have the shakes too badly to sit still.

On weekends, I usually go to Body Pump and/or hot yoga. I run most mornings. I go hiking here in North Carolina and as far out as the Smokies. I recently summited Mount Elbert in Colorado; the second tallest peak in the continental US. I go to the movies, I try new restaurants and I explore new parks. I look at the future, I make goals and I am able to complete those goals.

My heart is soft now. It is resilient. It can feel a punch without breaking from the impact. It is able to absorb the blow. It can contain the ripples, then it can bounce back. A hard heart can be broken by a punch, whether the punch is intentional or unintentional. A hard heart is fragile. I don't have to fear the punches anymore. People with both good and bad intentions will punch your heart. It's impossible to run from it without shutting off your heart. So I continue on a daily basis to make the choice to keep a soft heart and seek to become resilient instead of becoming untouchable. When you're untouchable, nobody can hurt you. But on that same note, you cannot experience love either. Because a guarded heart is shut off; it can't let the good in because the guards keep everything out.

My relationships are less volatile and fragile. They are open, meaningful and honest. I'm no longer guarded; I live vulnerably, with intention. I spend time engaged in intimate conversations with loved ones. My life has purpose; I am able to help people. I am able to be accountable for my actions. I am awake and aware of what I'm doing at all times.

Disapproval no longer kills me. Don't get me wrong, I like when people like me. But I don't live to avoid judgment. I actually love myself. Which is why I don't need to be loved or appreciated by every single person. My Heavenly Father's unending, merciful love completes me.

I can make eye contact. I can allow others, even strangers, to peer into my eyes and look at my soul because I don't feel the need to hide. I don't care if someone finds out who I am or what I do at night. The walls of my prison have dissolved and the world is my playground.

I am healed. I am whole.

Gina Mast
September 16 at 8:01 PM · 🌐

I came to Colorado to make Mt. Elbert (the second highest peak in the lower 48) my B... EAUtiful first 14er. Whether or not I will be able to walk tomorrow has yet to be determined.

Experiencing freedom. This mountain was a big moment for me. It was a gift from God. This trip was a customized answered prayer. I want others to know that they can not only be okay, but they can have their dreams come true too.

ENDING NOTE FROM THE AUTHOR

Everyone has a story. Your story can bring hope to the next person out there who is struggling right now. I want to share the resources I utilized, in case you need them. I'm a normal person without any formal writing experience. This means that if you want to, you can get your story out there too.

- I used www.Upwork.com to obtain copy editors, proofreaders, and photo editors.
  - Stephanie Larson was my primary editor. She was professional and easy to work with.
  - James Wilson edited my photos. He was responsive and worked quickly.
- I used www.DesignCrowd.com to have a logo made.
  - John C. Stefou designed my logo. He's communicative, creative, and pays attention to detail.
- I read Doug Addison's book *How to Write a Book Quickly* to learn everything you might need to know to write and publish a book. You can grab a copy at www.DougAddison.com.

You matter. Your story matters.

LOVE, LOVE, LOVE

I've been there.
I've made some bad choices.
But it does get better,
When you hear the right voices.

Regardless of your age,
Your current obstacles are new.
You're learning each day.
And you're gonna pull through.

Breath it all in,
Take it a day at a time.
And try to remember:
 Mistakes aren't a crime.

Some people act mean,
Because they don't understand.
Probably cause so far,
Life's given them the upper hand.

So what have I learned?
From my screw-ups and mistakes?
Grace can't be earned!
It's given to sinners and saints.

I'd rather learn young,
And live with humility,
Than have it all perfect,
And judge disability.

Some people smoke too much,

Hopelust

Drink too much,
Or dabble with drugs.
Others eat too much,
Preach too much,
Or sleep with lots of thugs (A thug is simply a violent person/criminal. I mean it as a general term for any person who isn't good for you).

Instead of pointing a finger,
Extend your full hand.
And help the next person,
Who's struggling to stand.

Wisdom will chase you,
Like wrinkles chase age.
Each day, you are new.
You don't live in a cage.

Your life isn't over.
Until you say it's done.
But even if you've given up,
You'll never lose the Son.

He'll keep fighting for you.
He'll keep showing you love.
And one day you'll realize,
You are loved from above.

Love, love, love.
F*** the rest.
Love, love, love.
Just do your best.

Copyright © 2015 by Regina Mast

www.ingramcontent.com/pod-product-compliance
Lightning Source LLC
LaVergne TN
LVHW052255070426
835507LV00035B/2911